# SHOREHAM AIRPORT SUSSEX

*T.M.A. Webb*

With best wishes
Tim Webb
Dennis L. Bird

This book is dedicated to Fred and George Miles, and to Cecil Pashley, who between them contributed so much to further the cause of aviation at Shoreham.

Also to Richard M. Almond, who would have written this book had he lived.

Published in 1996 by:
Cirrus Associates (S.W.),
Kington Magna,
Gillingham,
Dorset, SP8 5EW,
England.

ISBN 0 9515598 2 6


Photo scanning by:
Minet Scans Pty. Ltd.,
Boronia 3155, Australia.

Printed in England by:
Hillman Printers (Frome) Ltd.,
Frome, Somerset, BA11 4RW.

Sole Distributors to the UK book trade:
Cirrus Associates (S.W.),
Kington Magna,
Gillingham,
Dorset, SP8 5EW.

Cover photos
Miles Gemini G-AKKB by courtesy of
James Buckingham, and Bob Evans,
Bristol and West Photography.
Aerial photo of Shoreham: copyright
Chief Constable of Sussex.

# CONTENTS

# FOREWORD

## *By Grahame K. Gates, AFRAeS*

At last somebody has undertaken the formidable task of recording the long history of Shoreham Airport, one of the oldest airfields in the United Kingdom, and the oldest licensed one. Who better qualified to record it all than Tim Webb, an aviation enthusiast who grew up just before WW II on the hill overlooking the airfield. This project has been truly international, with Tim located in Australia, myself in Florida and many contributors in the UK, altogether an excellent example of international coordination, and all without the internet!

The history of Shoreham Airport has had six distinct phases: the pioneers prior to WW I, military use during WW I, the growth of private flying between the wars, military use during WW II, the Miles/Beagle years, and the growth of the last 25 years. Tim has recorded each of these in remarkable detail, particularly the pioneer years which are obviously much more difficult and time-consuming to research than more recent events. Dennis Bird has contributed to the work with well-researched material covering the later years.

Of the pioneer airfields, Shoreham is one of the very few to have survived, and airfields such as Hendon and Brooklands have long since closed, although Brooklands still has part of its runway for occasional fly-ins. Both of course have their museums to commemorate the past. Other airports such as Croydon have disappeared and new ones such as Heathrow have replaced them, but through it all Shoreham has continued to cater for the needs of general aviation and light military aviation for nearly ninety years, gradually developing, and getting larger. The distinctive terminal building is celebrating its 60th anniversary and the airfield now has its hard runway. The airport also boasts five maintenance facilities, eight flying clubs and several eateries, together with the headquarters of the Popular Flying Association.

Altogether a vast and welcome improvement over the Shoreham Airport where I worked for the Miles brothers and Beagle in 1951-64. I hope that it will continue to grow and prosper, catering for the needs of general aviation for many years to come.

Tim, many thanks for taking the trouble!

Grahame K. Gates,
Vero Beach, Florida.

3

# AUTHOR'S PREFACE

"The Shoreham Aviation Ground" started in 1910 just seven years after the Wright brothers first flew in 1903, so researching its history has been a monumental job as much of the story is now beyond living memory.

Most people reading this history will probably know where Shoreham Airport is located, but for those who do not, perhaps I should set the scene. Shoreham is on the flat coastal strip of the south coast of England in Sussex, between Brighton and Worthing. It is bounded by the South Downs to the north, and the River Adur to the east. The long embankment of the British Rail south coast railway is immediately to the south forming the southern boundary, and the English Channel is just a short distance further south.

My father, A.W.B. Webb, joined the staff at Lancing College in 1926, and I was born at our home in Hoe Court, North Lancing in 1929. We had a magnificent view over the aerodrome, and I was thus well placed to witness many of the events which occur in this history. As a young boy I watched the planes coming and going, and I can clearly remember the Southern Aircraft hangars on the old aerodrome to the west of New Salts Farm Road. Then came the advent of the new Municipal Airport, and the steady development up to 1939.

The war years forced my absence, but I was to return to the area post-war, and watched the recovery of Shoreham right up to 1959, when fate took me to Australia. Needless to say the tyranny of time and distance has proved a challenge, but remarkably, with the support of many people both in the U.K. and overseas, the story has gradually come together.

Necessarily the history has been built on surviving newspaper reports and magazine articles. The Public Records Office has yielded dates of WW II attacks on the airfield with details of the attacking aircraft and bombs dropped etc. The Operation Report Books of the airfield and squadrons stationed at Shoreham also provided useful information. Some detail from the original research material has had to be excluded in the interests of space. Students of history should refer to the excellent publications listed in the Bibliography. The story is presented in chronological order, year by year, and is split into four sections. Part 1 deals with the initial period from 1909 up to 1921. Part 2 covers the period in between the wars, while Part 3 is devoted to WW II and up to 1952. Part 4 is the work of Dennis L. Bird, and presents the main events in the period 1953-1996.

Of the more remarkable features of Shoreham's history are the many interesting characters who are woven into the fabric of the story. Like actors in a play they reappear at intervals or their progeny take up the story and history repeats itself. I refer of course to people like Cecil Pashley who first came to Shoreham with his brother Eric as long ago as 1911. Cecil was to survive two world wars as an instructor, returning to Shoreham after each war and continuing to teach people to fly until he retired at the age of 70.

Also there was Stanley F. Vincent, who as a young boy watched Shoreham's very first flier Harold Piffard make his early flights from Shoreham in 1910. Like Piffard, Vincent went to Lancing College, and became a pilot. He served as a Flight Commander with the Royal Flying Corps (RFC) at Shoreham in 1918. He again gets a mention in the 1940s during the Battle of Britain.

Two families in particular stand out. The first in order of appearance is the Gates family. Charles Gates enters the story in 1911 when as a schoolboy of fourteen he watched the early fliers at Shoreham. He went on to get a job as a carpenter there, and worked on many of the interesting planes built at Shoreham from 1912-1915. Serving in both the Royal Naval Air Service (RNAS) and later the Royal Air Force (RAF), in which he was commissioned as an Observer, he subsequently went out to Australia. He joined the RAAF in 1922, and specialised in the field of air radio. He reached the rank of Wing Commander before retirement in 1946, and then went on to a career in Government service.

4

Thirty-six years after Charles Gates left Shoreham, his nephew Grahame Gates also came to work there as an Aerodynamicist and Stressman for George Miles when F.G. Miles Ltd. was established at Shoreham in 1951. He had in fact begun his association with the Miles team in 1942 at Woodley.

The second family is of course the Miles family itself and its associates, who twice in a lifetime operated from Shoreham. Fred Miles, who persuaded Cecil Pashley to return to Shoreham after WW I, was a vital link in the eventual development of Shoreham Airport as this history will reveal. Fred's father, Frederick Gaston Miles, was persuaded to buy the land on which most of the present day airfield is situated. While the site would probably have been chosen by the local Councils in the long run, the Miles family were certainly a catalyst.

The boys of Lancing College which overlooks the airfield come into the narrative at frequent intervals. Like the author who was a pupil there from 1944-47, the airfield had a great influence on their lives, and many ended up in the RFC or RAF with distinguished careers.

Some of the photos used are admittedly of rather poor quality as the original negatives are no longer available. We have had to use old prints, and reproductions from old magazine photos in some cases.

Before closing I would be most remiss if I did not pay tribute to the late Richard Almond, a former member of the air traffic control staff at the Airport, who set out to record the history of Shoreham, but who sadly died in 1991 before he was able to complete his work. He left behind 17 large scrapbooks full of interesting material, much of which has been incorporated as he would have wished.

So I offer this history of Shoreham Airport, a much loved airfield which has survived for 86 years. It has known the smell of burnt castor oil and the wheezes of the early Renault and Gnome engines, the familiar beat of the Gipsy Major, the roar of Merlin engines of wartime Spitfires, and the whine of jet engines of the modern era.

It has seen success and failure, happiness and sadness, and yet through all it has continued to develop over the years, and today boasts modern facilities including an all-weather tarmac runway. The scene is ever-changing, and people come and go, but the larks still sing high overhead on summer days, and the air has that same salty tang from the River Adur which Piffard would have known. The Downs and Lancing College Chapel have remained the same backdrop to it all, silent witnesses to the passing years...

As with all such histories, despite my best endeavours errors or omissions may have occurred, and I would welcome advice on any detected.

T.M.A. Webb
April 1996.

# ACKNOWLEDGEMENTS

I have had the support of many people both in the UK and overseas, and in particular the following deserve my special thanks in order of contact:

Janet Pennington, Archivist at Lancing College, who responded to my initial inquiries with extracts on Shoreham Airport from the College archives, and who inspired me to undertake the task in the first place.

Roy Brooks, author of "Sussex Flights and Fliers 1783-1919", who provided a microfiche of his book on which much of Part 1 is based. He also provided useful material and made many helpful suggestions for Part 2.

Sylvia Adams, who was taught to fly by Cecil Pashley in 1956, and who is herself preparing a biography on the life of the Pashley Brothers. She has been most helpful with details from logbooks of Pashley's first Avro 504, and other unrecorded details of the early days of the Pashley/Miles partnership.

John Hopton, Aviation Historian of St. Kilda, Melbourne, who made available from his unique collection many of the books used in the research. He never failed to provide an answer for my many phone queries!

David Dunstall of The Shoreham Airport Collection for his enthusiasm and regular letters of support. His contributions have been of enormous value, and as "my man on the scene" at the Airport, he has always been ready to provide memorabilia to build up the story. I could not have done it without him.

My son Michael, who introduced me to the world of computers when I was long past the "Use By" date. His constant guidance in getting the history safely on to a computer disk has been invaluable. In the later stages, my eldest son, Stephen, also became involved in transferring the whole story on to more compatible disks. I owe them both a great debt.

Norm Lumley, pilot and light aircraft owner in Melbourne, whose many contacts in the aviation world in Australia provided early leads to the Charles Gates story, and to Gary Sunderland, of Ballarat, Victoria, for providing copies of an interview with Charles Gates recorded in Australia in 1984.

Grahame Gates, nephew of Charles Gates. Grahame is now residing in Florida USA where he worked for Piper after leaving Beagle at Shoreham in 1964. He has provided a wealth of material relating to his uncle, including tape recordings and copies of correspondence. Unique amongst the records are photos of Charles Gates and the Gates-Wallis plane. His advice and consultation on the Miles/Beagle story has been invaluable.

Former Aircraftman Alfred Gitter of 277 Squadron, for his personal memories of D-Day in 1944.

Peter Amos of the Miles Aircraft Collection for supplying details of F.G. Miles' early log book entries, and unravelling the early post WW I days at Shoreham.

Richard S. Robinson, Military Aviation Historian, for research into the Public Record Office data, and acknowledgement is made for the use of Crown copyright material.

The staff at the RAAF Museum at Point Cook, Victoria for allowing me access to early copies of "Aero", "Flight", and "The Aeroplane" held in their archives. These contained many interesting articles and photos of early Shoreham now incorporated into the story.

Stuart Leslie, North Yorkshire, for seeking out from his Collection some marvellous photos of Shoreham in the period from 1910 to 1919.

Flt. Lt. Keith Lohan (retd), former Mustang pilot in 231 Squadron, and C.O. of The London University Auxiliary Squadron at Shoreham in 1946-47, for wartime details and photos of the 1947 era.

Former pupils of Lancing College who responded to my call for help in the Lancing Club

Newsletter. They included J.C. Sprent, L.K.W. Williams, Dr. George Cross, Gordon Flex and Dr. Robin Kimmerling.

Former Lancing College pupil and author, Peter G. Campbell, who has also written two books which feature Shoreham Airport in the 1950s (see the Bibliography), for the very considerable help and advice he gave on the road to publication. His continual enthusiasm for the whole project never faltered. In particular the very considerable skill he displayed in the final proof-reading of the entire manuscript by fax deserves the highest praise.

C.L. Chamberlin, my Godfather and former Master at Lancing College, who taught me English over 50 years ago. At over 90 years of age he kindly undertook to read the manuscript, and quickly reminded me about aspects of punctuation and grammar long since forgotten . . . (Sadly, he died on February 21st 1996, only a few weeks after completing his work on the manuscript).

Lewis "Benjy" Benjamin, founder of the Brookside Flying Group which operated at Shoreham from 1948-1950, for his anecdotes of that period including the story of "Drunken Davis".

Former Aircraftman Sydney Holden of RAF Shoreham who provided a vivid account of the German air raid on the night of February 13th 1943 when over 1000 incendiaries were dropped.

Mike F. Williams, Researcher of The Shoreham Airport Collection, for copies of his comprehensive records of RAF Shoreham 1941-1944, and RAF Regiment details which filled in many blanks.

Sqn. Ldr. Dennis L. Bird (retd.) for much useful background material from the Air Historical Branch, and for the use of items in his article "RAF Shoreham, 1940-45...a Schoolboy's Memories" in the "Shoreham Herald" of August 22nd and 29th 1975. In addition, to him my special thanks for the suggestion of an Epilogue to cover the period 1953-1996. In his hands, that Epilogue grew dramatically and finally became Part 4 of this book with four chapters in its own right.

F/O Bert Watson (retd.) of 277 Squadron for the recollections and excerpts from his personal records which have proved very helpful. Much of his chapter from "Odd Bods At War" has been included.

Neil Follett, of Abaronet Studios in Chirnside Park, Melbourne, for his constant support and co-operation on the reproduction of the many photos.

June Lagalisse in Canada for making available her records of 345 Free French Squadron, and the personal memories of her late husband, Charles Lagalisse.

Chris Corcoran and all the staff at Snap Printing in Ringwood, Victoria, for their unfailing good service, and for the many "specials" such as the maps in this book.

Don Box and Staff at Minet Scans Pty Ltd. who so ably scanned all the photos and prepared the colour cover.

Joel Hands, my elder grandson, who at 17 years of age has the computer world at his finger tips; my special thanks for coming to the rescue when my computer broke down at the eleventh hour midway through inputting the captions for all the photos. With both grandfather and grandson working simultaneously on two of his computers, we just made it!

Peter R. March, Aviation Journalist, who at the last moment very kindly assisted with further data on the Beagle Basset story.

Last but by no means least, to Mickie my wife, my grateful thanks for putting up with nearly three years of being an "aviation golf widow", and all too often hearing the sounds of exasperation when the "computer operator" hit the wrong key and the latest input got erased!

T.M.A.W.

## AERODROME BOUNDARIES

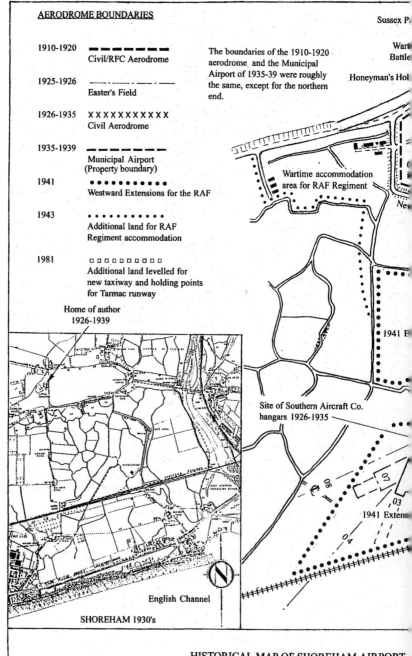

**1910-1920**
▬ ▬ ▬ ▬ ▬ ▬ ▬
Civil/RFC Aerodrome

**1925-1926**
▬ · ▬ · ▬ · ▬ · ▬
Easter's Field

**1926-1935**
X X X X X X X X X X X X
Civil Aerodrome

**1935-1939**
▬ ▬ ▬ ▬ ▬ ▬ ▬
Municipal Airport
(Property boundary)

**1941**
● ● ● ● ● ● ● ● ● ● ●
Westward Extensions for the RAF

**1943**
● · ● · ● · ● · ● · ●
Additional land for RAF
Regiment accommodation

**1981**
▢ ▢ ▢ ▢ ▢ ▢ ▢ ▢ ▢
Additional land levelled for
new taxiway and holding points
for Tarmac runway

Home of author
1926-1939

The boundaries of the 1910-1920
aerodrome and the Municipal
Airport of 1935-39 were roughly
the same, except for the northern
end.

Sussex P

War
Battle

Honeyman's Hol

Wartime accommodation
area for RAF Regiment

Ne

1941 E

Site of Southern Aircraft Co.
hangars 1926-1935

80
07
03
1941 Extens
04

English Channel

SHOREHAM 1930's

## HISTORICAL MAP OF SHOREHAM AIRPORT

Based on 1943 map with modern runway layout sup
for reference. Scale 1/2500

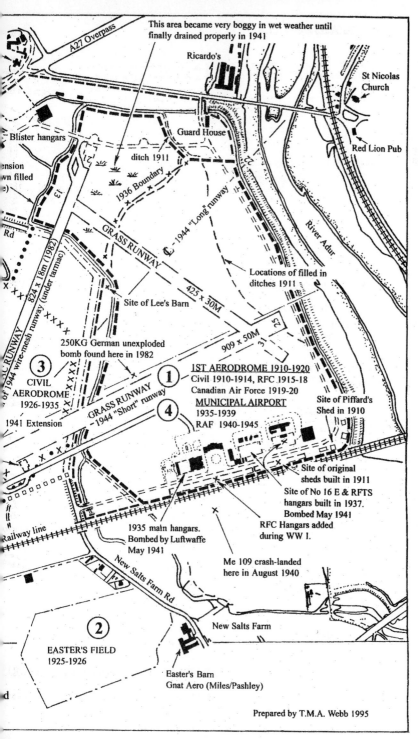

This area became very boggy in wet weather until finally drained properly in 1941

Ricardo's

St Nicolas Church

A27 Overpass

Blister hangars

Guard House

Red Lion Pub

ditch 1911

ension
wn filled
e)

1936 Boundary

Rd

1944 "Long" runway

GRASS RUNWAY

River Adur

Locations of filled in ditches 1911

425 x 30M

824 x 18m (1982) wire-mesh runway (under tarmac)

Site of Lee's Barn

909 x 50M

25

31

250KG German unexploded bomb found here in 1982

(3)
CIVIL
AERODROME
1926-1935

1944 wire-mesh runway

GRASS RUNWAY
1944 "Short" runway

(1)

1ST AERODROME 1910-1920
Civil 1910-1914, RFC 1915-18
Canadian Air Force 1919-20

Site of Piffard's
Shed in 1910

1941 Extension

(4)

MUNICIPAL AIRPORT
1935-1939
RAF 1940-1945

Site of original
sheds built in 1911

Site of No 16 E & RFTS
hangars built in 1937.
Bombed May 1941
RFC Hangars added
during WW I.

Railway line

1935 main hangars.
Bombed by Luftwaffe
May 1941

Me 109 crash-landed
here in August 1940

New Salts Farm Rd

New Salts Farm

(2)

EASTER'S FIELD
1925-1926

Easter's Barn
Gnat Aero (Miles/Pashley)

d

Prepared by T.M.A. Webb 1995

2A

# Part 1 (1909–1921)

## Chapter 1    THE EARLY YEARS (1909–1914)

### 1909

Late in 1909 George Arthur Wingfield, a solicitor, took out a six month lease from the farmer at New Salts Farm who owned land on what is now the south-east corner of the present airfield. Wingfield had just set up his fledgling company called Aviators Finance Co. Ltd., after forming an association with one Harold Hume Piffard, an artist, who also had a hobby building model planes! This had led to Piffard building a full size aeroplane in 1909 at North Ealing, and which he flew late that year at Hanger Hill. Sadly it was then wrecked in a storm which demolished both plane and hangar.

### 1910

Undaunted, Piffard or "Piff," as he was affectionately known to his companions, set out to build a second machine. Shoreham was selected as a suitable site, and a shed forty foot square was erected in the south-east corner of the field, just opposite the end of the railway bridge.

No doubt Piffard was attracted to the site having been a pupil at nearby Lancing College (1877-83). The second aircraft was similar to the first, rather like a Bristol Boxkite, being a pusher biplane with a front elevator and a rear stabiliser. It was powered by a 40 h.p. ENV engine with a seven foot diameter propeller.

The new aircraft was ready by May 1910, and had its first "hop" that month.  To mark the occasion Piffard was invited to lunch at Lancing College as a somewhat distinguished old boy.

At the time land available for take-off and landing was very limited as the area was very swampy, and crisscrossed by numerous drainage ditches. A high bank known as "the tow path" separated the River Adur from the field, and a system of gates was cut into the bank to allow the field to be drained at low tide. Even the one good length had a ditch midway which had to be boarded over. A red flag was placed at each end to identify it from the air!

Initial flights were in a straight line on calm days, and mostly from south to north. The aircraft had to be turned round at the end of each flight. Piffard then flew back to the starting point. To encourage his efforts the Landlord at the nearby Sussex Pad Inn offered Piffard a crate of champagne if he could fly over and collect it!

Piffard gradually gained confidence, but before he could learn to make turns the machine was caught by a gust of wind at thirty feet causing him to crash. While Piffard was not hurt, the machine was badly damaged, and it was June before it was repaired. The first recorded proper flight was achieved on July 10th 1910.

In August a young Stanley Vincent, later to become a pupil at Lancing College and a pilot himself, was on holiday with his parents, and spent hours watching Piffard. Vincent's father was a Doctor of Music, and he used his tuning fork to help Piffard tune his engine! (The origin of the term "tune-up").

Piffard continued flying, but was repeatedly plagued by bad weather and structural failures. The engine also gave him problems, and cylinders had to be changed. On one occasion he damaged his propeller breaking off one tip. The missing part was found and re-attached, somewhat crudely, and balanced by fitting bolts to the opposite blade! It appears to have worked, and of course in those days there were no regulations! Piffard gradually improved his skills, and on September 11th 1910 he was making some good controlled flights; so as the weather was good he flew over to the Sussex Pad Inn to collect his champagne from a Landlord who probably thought he would never have to honour the challenge!

Piffard went on to perfect his techniques, but his attempts to make turns always ended in a crash

8

and so far as is known he never managed a circuit. However he had plenty of admiring audiences, and one day Pathé Frères of "Pathé Gazette" appeared with a cine-camera. Piffard prepared to take off over one of the ditches about one hundred and fifty yards away, telling Pathé he would be airborne well before reaching the ditch. However he overlooked the tailwind, and promptly ended up in the ditch. The delighted Pathé had a sooop for "Pathé Gazette" news, and for weeks after Piffard found himself on the screen of the local cinemas!

Then in October Piffard had another bad crash in his "Humming Bird", as it was known locally, and although he escaped more or less unhurt, the machine was beyond repair. However Piffard had established himself in history as the first person to build and fly an aircraft at Shoreham. The engine, rudder and propeller are preserved to this day in the Science Museum in South Kensington, London.

He did go on to design and build "Humming Bird" Mk II, but this time it was a hydro biplane or seaplane and was built in London in 1911. It was brought to Shoreham beach near the Good Shepherd Church for trials, but it proved to be troublesome and would not unstick. At the end of 1911 it was wrecked in a storm, and thereafter Piffard ran out of money for his aviation exploits. So he probably returned to being an artist, having become quite well known as a painter of scenes from military events. He lived to be seventy-two and died in 1938.

In 1951, Air Marshall Stanley Vincent, CB, DFC and AFC (the same Stanley Vincent who had watched Piffard in 1910), wrote a tribute to Piffard in the Golden Jubilee issue of the Royal Aero Club journal.

## *1911*

On March 7th 1911, Oscar Morison landed his Bleriot monoplane at Shoreham after a flight from Brighton where he had been for two weeks making demonstration flights. Aged twenty-seven, Morison had already established himself among the early aviators, and he had obtained his Royal Aero Club Brevet No. 46 in January 1911. He made Shoreham his base, and it appears he had no lack of funds, having already survived several crashes and spending considerable sums on repairs. (Morison with two "r"s is quoted in the 1913 edition of "Janes All The World's Aircraft", but this may be in error as all the contemporary press reports, magazines and photos used the less common "Morison").

On March 11th 1911 Morison was invited to visit Lancing College by the Head Master, the Rev. H.T. Bowlby. Morison flew up and circled the Chapel at 1000 feet, and then landed on the cricket pitch. The very smooth turf did not slow him up as fast as usual, and he slightly damaged his machine on the rising ground known as the Grubber bank. Morison left his mechanic to repair the Bleriot, and flew it back to Shoreham the next day, where it was kept in Piffard's old shed.

The local press had already reported on Morison's arrival in the area, and the "The Daily Graphic" of March 1st 1911Δ also featured a map of the proposed "Brighton and Hove Aerodrome". The Editor of the Lancing College Magazine at the time was E.B. Gordon, and Morison's visit was the subject of the Editorial in the April 1911 issue. Many years later E.B. Gordon would learn to fly at Shoreham himself.

On April 15th, Morison had yet another accident when he crashed his Bleriot at Eastbourne, but again he survived.

Wingfield and his airfield manager Pettit began to develop Shoreham as a leading aerodrome, filling in some of the ditches to provide a landing run of some two thousand feet north to south. Its borders were roughly the same as the later Municipal Airport of 1935-1939, the ditches forming natural boundaries. (See location No. 1 on the Historical Map).

Shoreham was nominated as a turning point for the Brooklands to Brighton Air Race on May 6th 1911, which the "Sussex Daily News" hailed as "a race which would go down to posterity as the first aerial point-to-point race". The contestants included some well known fliers of the time: Graham Gilmour (Bristol Boxkite), Howard Pixton (Avro Biplane), Lt. Snowden Smith (Farman), and Gustav

Hamel (Bleriot). Morison did not take part in the race as his machine had been damaged. Most of the competitors either got disqualified or lost their way, and Gustav Hamel was declared the winner! Gustav Hamel had in fact learnt to fly in France in 1910, and was a holder of R.A.E. certificate 64 which he obtained in February 1911.

Morison also had a Bristol Boxkite at Shoreham which he used for joy flights after the air race. The first passenger ever to fly from Shoreham was a Mr. E.W. Carr who took off with Morison at 4.20 p.m. on May 7th 1911, and the event was duly recorded in the "Sussex Daily News" next day. He also took up a Mrs. Buller, wife of the Chairman of the Shoreham and Lancing Land Company. Also among his early passengers was a Boy Scout named Digby Cleaver of the First Shoreham Troop, who was in fact the first Scout to fly. The charge for these early passenger flights from Shoreham was £5, which was quite a considerable fee for the times.

On May 13th there was yet another race, this time from Shoreham to Black Rock, East Brighton. However there were only two competitors - Gilmour and Morison. Morison just won, but Gilmour rather stole the limelight by then landing on the tennis courts at nearby Roedean Girls' School. He was joined moments later by Morison much to the delight of the girls!

On June 20th 1911, the newly titled Brighton and Shoreham Aerodrome was officially opened at a luncheon attended by local dignitaries including the Mayors of Brighton, Hove and Worthing. Managing Director and Chairman George Wingfield, and his airfield manager W. Pettit had by this time succeeded in attracting several companies to the aerodrome including the British Colonial Aeroplane Company, and one Gordon England who also operated a Boxkite at Shoreham for a short while. In later years Gordon England was to become well known for the design and testing of several types at Shoreham.

Initially about six hangars (or sheds as they were called then) were established at Shoreham built in a row just below the railway line, but much closer to it than today's buildings, and to the east of the Terminal Building. Piffard's shed was still on site, but while initially they used it as a hangar, for some reason it was then converted into the Aerodrome Restaurant which appears in many photos. Then in 1912 they built a pavilion for the Brighton-Shoreham Aero Club next to the Restaurant. The Shoreham Flying School provided instruction using Bristol Boxkites situated in shed No. 3.

Not all the sheds were occupied at first. For a while a Metzar-Leno monoplane, minus engine but with a beautiful gull wing, sat in shed No. 4, and a Wright glider was in No. 5 shed. It appears the Metzar-Leno monoplane only made a few hops, and never really flew from Shoreham before being removed.

Basil H. England (not related to Gordon England) and an associate named Collyer occupied shed No. 6. They operated a small flying school, but the pupils were largely self-taught. They also built their Collyer-England biplane fitted with a 30 h.p. Alvaston engine. It was later modified with a 35 h.p. Green engine. However it does not appear to have been very successful, only making short flights and limited turns.

On July 4th 1911, Horatio Barber flew with the world's first recorded air freight. He flew from Shoreham to Hove with a consignment of Osram lamps for the Electric Congress organised by the General Electric Light Co., and landed safely at the Marine Park, in Wish Road. The aircraft was the Valkyrie B tail-first canard two-seater, powered by a 50 h.p. Gnome engine. He designed and built the machine himself, and was awarded a fee of £100 for the flight. To commemorate his flight two roads at the Heathrow Cargo Terminal are named "Shoreham East" and "Shoreham West".

The Circuit of Europe Air Race had started from Paris on June 18th 1911, with forty-three contestants, and the route went through France, Belgium, Holland and Britain. Contestants passed through Shoreham en route, but it was to be August 7th before the last stragglers made it. The only English competitors, Morison and Valentine, both failed on the first leg in France. Morison crashed (again) and Valentine force-landed.

10

Early in July the Circuit of Britain Air Race was also organised with seventeen entrants. Once again early Shoreham identities took part: Morison, Gilmour and England. S.F. Cody, the first man to fly from Farnborough, also took part. The route began at Hendon, then went to Edinburgh in the north, and passed through Carlisle and Manchester to Exeter in the south, and then finally to Brooklands via Shoreham.

Wingfield saw the race as an opportunity to cash in on crowds watching the event. He had a long corrugated iron fence erected along the top of the tow path, and right along the northern boundary to the Sussex Pad. He wanted to prevent spectators sitting on the bank instead of paying an entrance fee! However it was a dismal failure as most people could see quite well from the surrounding high ground, and he earned adverse publicity from the local press for "vandalism". The fence remained for many years, and readily identified the background as Shoreham in early photos.

On July 8th 1911, Morison made the first flight from Paris to Shoreham in his newly bought Morane Borel racing monoplane which he had intended to use in the Circuit of Europe Air Race on June 18th, but the machine was not ready in time. His flight time from Paris to Shoreham was a little over 12 hours via Calais, Dover and Eastbourne. A week later Morison was to have his most spectacular crash when he rashly tried to land the Morane downwind at Brooklands, and cartwheeled. He was lucky to escape uninjured. In September he was to force-land his Bleriot in the sea off the Isle of Wight, and while he was rescued, and the plane salvaged, it was the end of his flying days. In November 1912 he married Margaret Cleaver, sister of the Boy Scout Digby Cleaver, and it seems she kept him earthbound thereafter . . .

On July 24th 1911, there was a unusual race. Claude Grahame-White, in a Farman pusher seaplane named "Wake Up England", challenged local hotelier Harry Preston in a fifty-five foot motor cruiser over a course from Black Rock, Brighton to Portslade. Although Grahame-White had to make two laps to Preston's one, the Farman won by ten yards.

On August 6th, Horatio Barber was back at Shoreham with a Miss Trehawke Davies who had a reputation for living dangerously. She had persuaded Barber to fly her from Hendon to Shoreham and back. By all accounts the journey was full of incidents, and at one point Barber was forced to make an emergency landing near Steyning, just five miles north of the aerodrome when he ran low in fuel, and was being forced backwards by the wind!

The French Deperdussin Co. also set up their English representative at Shoreham, Lt. J.C. Porter.

Around this time it is probable that the Pashley Brothers first visited Shoreham although no actual date is known. Cecil Pashley had gained his Brevet No. 106 in July 1911, and Eric Pashley gained his, No. 139, in the September of 1911 (both were self-taught). So it is quite possible that they could have visited Shoreham in the last half of 1911, in the course of joyriding flights out of Brooklands to Shoreham which it is known they were making soon after gaining their Brevets. (The first photo of them at Shoreham was taken in 1912).

Then in November 1911, the Chanter Flying School moved to Shoreham from Hendon and occupied sheds No. 7 and 8. They had two Bleriots, and began instructing pupils. Chanter had himself designed and built a small Nieuport type monoplane which flew from Hendon in that year. This machine also came to Shoreham.

## 1912

One of Shoreham's earliest pilots, Graham Gilmour, was killed on February 17th 1912, when he lost the left wing of his Martin Handasyde at four hundred feet over Richmond Park after taking off from Brooklands for Hendon in turbulent conditions.

The Chanter Flying School was now well established with half a dozen pilots under training. Among them was a Swiss engineer, Emile Gasser, who hoped to become an aircraft designer.

Another new arrival at Shoreham was Lt. Lawrence with a new Blackburn monoplane, and test flying of the Collyer/England biplane was proceeding.

# SHOREHAM'S FIRST AEROPLANE, THE PIFFARD BIPLANE OF 1910

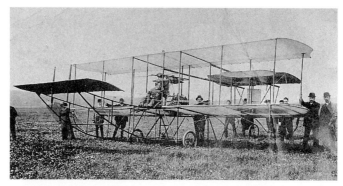

Harold Piffard in his Biplane at Shoreham in 1910. He designed and built the machine, and then taught himself to fly. He made the first flight on July 10th 1910.

Photo: JMB/GSL Collection.

Another view of Piffard's Biplane with the railway bridge over the River Adur in the background. This photo provided the first clue on the exact location of Piffard's original shed which can just be seen on the extreme right. It was later converted into the Aerodrome Restaurant.

Photo: JMB/GSL Collection.

Although of poor quality, this unique photo of Piffard's Biplane in flight was taken looking to the south-east with Piffard's shed and the railway behind. Smoke from a passing train is thought to be drifting down behind Piffard's shed obscuring the railway bridge.

Both these photos appeared in the May 1968 issue of "Sussex Life, the Country Magazine" in an article by E.M. Sutton entitled "The First Man to Fly Over Sussex".
Via Grahame Gates.

Piffard in his studio at North Ealing where many of the parts for his machines were made before assembly at Shoreham.

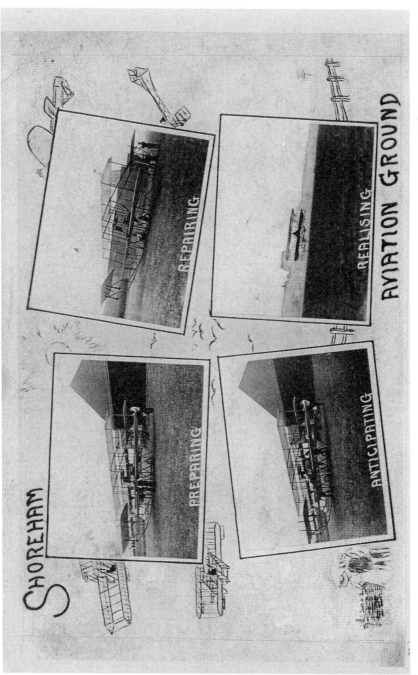

Four photos from a postcard of the times. By courtesy of Frank "Boots" Dorey.

# THE PIFFARD HYDROPLANE AT SHOREHAM BEACH IN 1912

The Hydroplane during assembly at Shoreham beach. Note the ski-board type floats which later proved so troublesome.

Right:
Barbara Blank, one of Piffard's art students, standing by the engine and radiator installation.
Bottom:
A very much modified version on Bungalow Town beach. Note the long front boom and the reduced lower wing; doubtless attempts to reduce the tendency to dig-in on acceleration.

All photos: JMB/GSL Collection

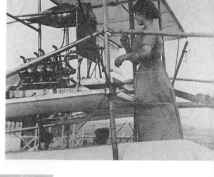

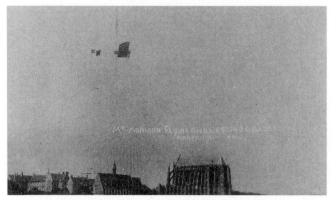

Oscar Morison in his Bleriot over Lancing College on March 11th 1911.
Photo: The Shoreham Airport Collection.

Morison's Bleriot being wheeled to Piffard's shed after his flight.
Photo: Edward Colquhoun Collection.

Morison flying his Bristol Boxkite at Shoreham in May 1911.
Photo: Terry Child's Collection, West Sussex County Council Library Service.

Morison with his Bleriot at Shoreham in May 1911.
Photo: Terry Child's Collection, West Sussex County Council Library Service.

A Maurice Farman "Longhorn" coming into land in 1911, against a backdrop which was to
become familiar over the years.
Photo: Edward Colquhoun Collection.

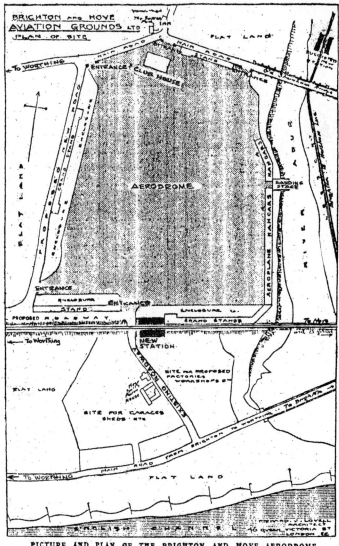

PICTURE AND PLAN OF THE BRIGHTON AND HOVE AERODROME.

Reproduced from an article in "The Daily Graphic" of March 1st 1911. This rather ambitious plan, which includes both a Grand Stand and some spectators' enclosures, also shows a row of hangars along the River Adur frontage. Note the new road replacing New Salts Farm Road on the western boundary. New stations were planned on both the adjacent railways, but only the Bungalow Town halt ever eventuated. Interestingly, at the top of the map there is the name "Brighton and Hove Aviation Grounds Ltd." However, it would seem that it had no connection with Wingfield. The London architect, J. Lovell, who prepared the map, could not have done much research on the site, as he placed the "Club House" almost in the notorious deep pond known as Honeyman's Hole! (see Appendix).

# SEASIDE FLIGHTS.

## THE NEW BRIGHTON AND HOVE AERODROME.

## A GORDON-BENNETT RUMOUR

Brighton for the past week has been entertaining her first visitor to arrive by air, in the person of Mr. O. C. Morrison, who safely landed upon the beach at Kemptown after a surprise flight from Brooklands. The aviator is now stormbound, and his 50 h.p. Gnome Blériot is causing great interest among the visitors and residents who have inspected it in its temporary home in a local garage.

When the present gale has blown itself cut—and to judge by the "glass" this will not be for some days—the Blériot will be wheeled along the front to the Hove lawns, and from this spot Mr. Morrison intends to fly to Brighton and Hove's new aviation ground, where during the coming summer the town hopes to have the pleasure of receiving all the best of the air's conquerors.

The new ground is situated between Brighton and Worthing, in a locality known as New Salts Farm, and covers an area of 320 acres. When everything is taken into consideration with regard to the position and surroundings, one is inclined to say that the ground is a very close approach to the ideal. On the east side runs the River Adur and the railway line from London via Horsham to Brighton; on the north it is bounded by the Old Shoreham Road, which will provide numerous entrances to the aerodrome; while on the south side runs the railway between Brighton and Worthing, the main road, and the English Channel.

A new station has been built on the ground between Brighton and Worthing, and another is to be erected at the opposite end of the aerodrome on the Horsham line. The London, Brighton Railway Company are giving the promoters every support, and have promised to run visitors from London to the aerodrome in one and a quarter hours without a change. The course will measure six miles, and this without a solitary tree in sight. Further sheds and workshops are to be erected, and a club-house is to be built during the spring.

Mr. Vallentine, who flies a passenger-carrying machine of his own design, has decided to make the new ground his headquarters, and during the summer will conduct a series of week-end trips between Brooklands and Brighton—a distance of thirty-four miles—via Leatherhead, Dorking, and Horsham. The railway line will make a splendid guide, and prevent any chance of the machine and its occupants arriving at some rival seaside resort by mistake. Mr. Vallentine's spare time is to be given to perfecting a machine of English make which will land and rise from the sea, so that he could not have chosen a better ground for his work.

Brighton is hoping that French aviators will visit her, and if they do not fly over their machines can be brought to Shoreham Harbour and up the River Adur to the ground. An interesting rumour is afloat in Brighton connecting the new aerodrome and the Gordon-Bennett Cup race. It is only natural that everyone in the town is keen on this prospect, and would do all in their power to make it a success. If the great race should happen to be flown on the new course the public can rest assured that they will be able to get there more quickly and with more comfort than they would to several of the aerodromes situated much nearer London.

W. I. V.

From the "Daily Graphic" Wednesday March 1st 1911.

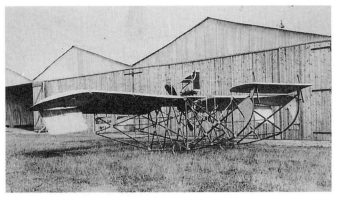

The Metzgar and Leno pusher monoplane at Shoreham in 1911.
Photo: JMB/GSL Collection.

The Collyer-England biplane in 1911 with a 30 h.p. Alvaston.
Photo: C.F. Andrews.

Horatio Barber and his Valkerie B pusher monoplane in which he carried the world's first air freight of Osram lamps from Shoreham to Hove on July 4th 1911.
Photo: JMB/GSL Collection.

This view, taken about 1912, shows Piffard's shed on the left converted into the Restaurant, and the Sussex County Aero Club pavilion on the right. The aerodrome manager's office can just be seen on the extreme left.
Photo: The Shoreham Airport Collection.

The view looking west from the pavilion with the hangars in the background. Note the tennis court.
Photo: Edward Colquhoun Collection.

# THE SHOREHAM AERODROME 1910 - 1914
## (Locations of the buildings of period)

| | Shed No. | TENANTS |
|---|---|---|
| **1911** | 3 | Shoreham Flying School |
| | 4 and 5 | Bristol Aeroplane Co. |
| | 6 | B.H. England School of Flying |
| | 7 and 8 | Chanter School of Flying |
| **1912** | 3 and 4 | Avro Works and Flying School |
| | 5, 6 and 7 | James Radley Works |
| **1913** | 3 and 4 | Avro/Pashley Bros. |
| | 5,6,7 | Shoreham School of Flying |
| | 8,9,10 | Cedric Lee |
| | | Private use. |
| **1914** | 5 | Pashley Bros. & Hale |
| | 6,7,8 | Cedric Lee |
| | 9,10 | Private use. |

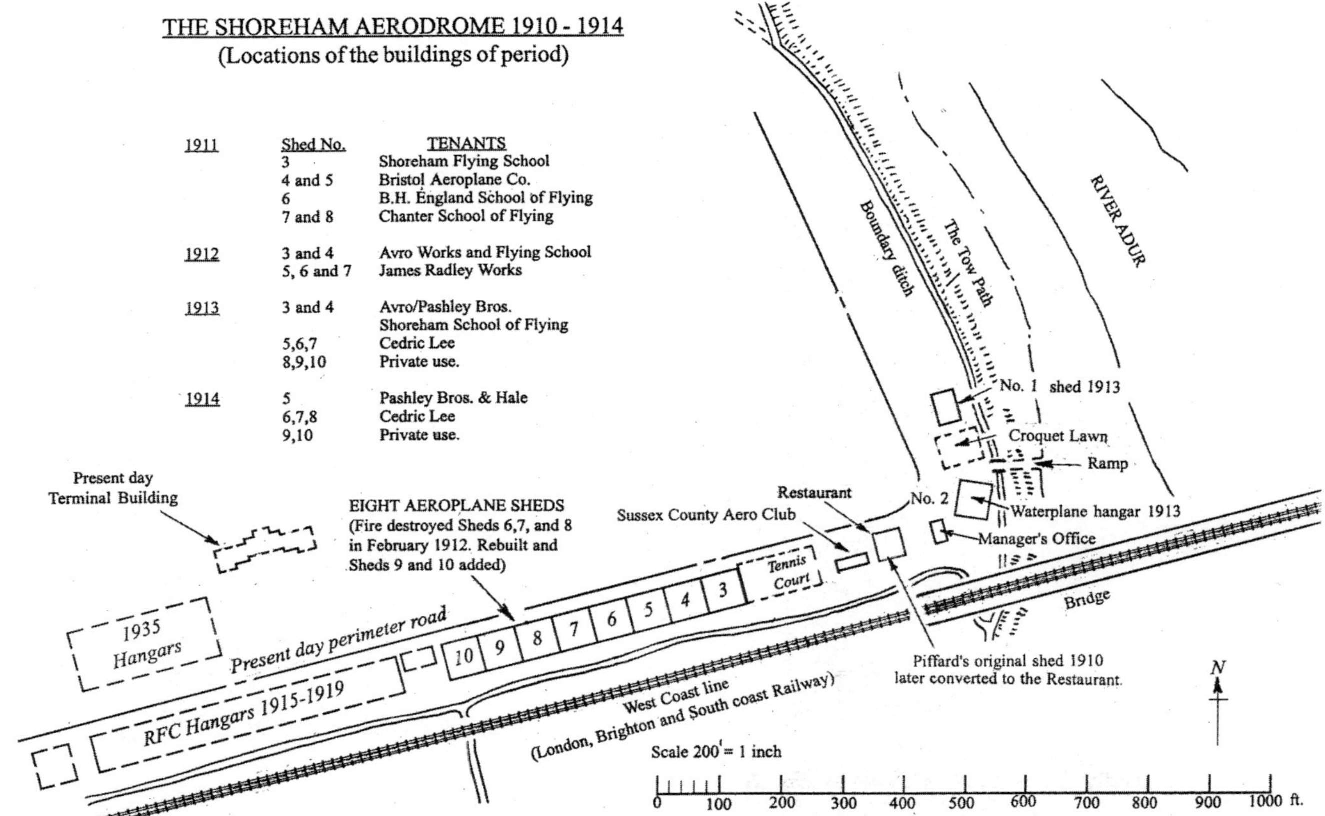

**EIGHT AEROPLANE SHEDS**
(Fire destroyed Sheds 6,7, and 8 in February 1912. Rebuilt and Sheds 9 and 10 added)

Present day Terminal Building

1935 Hangars

Present day perimeter road

RFC Hangars 1915-1919

RIVER ADUR

The Tow Path

Boundary ditch

No. 1 shed 1913

Croquet Lawn

Ramp

Waterplane hangar 1913

Manager's Office

No. 2

Bridge

Restaurant

Sussex County Aero Club

Tennis Court

3 4 5 6 7 8 9 10

West Coast line

(London, Brighton and South coast Railway)

Scale 200' = 1 inch

Piffard's original shed 1910 later converted to the Restaurant.

N

0 100 200 300 400 500 600 700 800 900 1000 ft.

T.W. 7/95

**Shed numbering**  The allocation of No. 3 to the first shed in the row no doubt stems from Piffards shed being the first building, and later converted to the Restaurant. Logically the Sussex County Aero Club Pavilion became No. 2.

**Note:** Additional sheds were added on the eastern boundary in 1912-13, and were then allocated No 1 and No 2. However No 1 shed had gone by 1914 ... maybe another fire?

About this time James Radley set up his Works at Shoreham in shed No. 5, and one of his first jobs was the modified Bleriot XI racing monoplane built for Will Rhodes-Moorhouse (later to become the RFC's first Victoria Cross holder).

Then late on the night of February 29th 1912, disaster struck. Fire broke out, and despite the best efforts of Flying Club members who did manage to drag some planes clear, at least three hangars were destroyed. It is believed the fire started in shed No. 8 at the end of the row, but the cause was never fully determined. A spark from a passing steam train may have been the culprit.

This spelt the end of the Chanter Flying School. The hangars were rebuilt, but there was a dispute with the builder which ended up in court. (The use of the word "hangar" rather than shed appears to have been adopted around this time.)

The Brighton and Shoreham aerodrome had a bad patch at this time, also losing a court action against Horatio Barber for a sum of £65 and unpaid fees associated with his flight with the Osram lamps.

On June 8th, Will Rhodes-Moorhouse came third in the first Aerial Derby at Hendon flying the Radley-Moorhouse monoplane, as the modified Bleriot was known.

There were new visitors to Shoreham. One of them was a Pierre Verrier who was only twenty-two. He flew his Maurice Farman Longhorn from Hendon to Shoreham, and then to Portsmouth where he flew over the Royal Review of the fleet before returning to Hendon.

Other visitors included a Frenchman, a Monsieur Salmet with a 70 h.p. Gnome Bleriot, and Gustav Hamel and Robert Slack both flying 80 h.p. Morane Saulnier monoplanes. Also A.E. Geere who gained Certificate No. 310 that year. Along with other early aerodromes like Brooklands and Hendon, Shoreham was rapidly becoming a popular destination for the early fliers.

Not all the personalities who contributed to the early history of Shoreham were fliers. Some were involved in the construction of the interesting planes of the times. One such person was Charles Gates who lived to be over ninety, but still had vivid recollections of early Shoreham, and clearly remembered the arrival of Oscar Morison over Brighton in 1911.

His memory was quite remarkable, and during an interview in 1984 he was able to recall and confirm much of the history of the period 1910-1915. As a schoolboy he used to spend his leisure hours watching the early fliers at Shoreham, and witnessed the stragglers of the 1911 Circuit of Europe who landed there. In the same year he saw Horatio Barber land back at Shoreham after his first carriage of aerial freight.

In 1912 at the age of fifteen, young Charles Gates, who was a skilled woodworker, got his first job with the B.H. England Flying School at Shoreham aerodrome for just five shillings (25p) a week! One of his first jobs was carving out the propeller for the "Tong Mei" biplane designed by an Australian-born Chinese gentleman by the name of Tsoe K. Wong. Charles Gates spent many hours working on the propeller carving it out of solid N.Z. Kauri. There was a 40 h.p. ENV engine in the hangar which was to be fitted to the plane, and Charles believed it came from Piffard's first plane.

Wong had been sent to England to learn the latest technology, and return with it to China. He gained an engineering qualification in England, and was learning to fly the Collyer-England biplane. He had several escapades while learning to fly, and as Charles Gates observed, "in those days there was no formal instruction. It was rather like learning to ride a bicycle, and eventually you fell off!" One day Wong started a fast run towards the hangars from the northern end of the airfield, and about 150 yards short of the hangars he throttled back sharply, causing his tail to drop, and he executed a left-hand climbing turn before landing back facing the opposite direction quite unharmed!

However one day he rashly tried to fly the Collyer-England biplane over the sheds, but crashed in the attempt. This ended his association with B.H. England, and it seems he then departed with his unfinished "Tong Mei". The photo in the following pages shows a two-seater version which was a later development possibly built for him by Boulton and Paul. Wong finished his flying training at Brooklands, and eventually set up an aviation service in Malaya using Avro 504s. Shortly after Wong left, B.H. England closed his Flying School, and later joined the RNAS as an Engineer Officer.

In October a new aerodrome Manager, Mr. H. Gonne, took over and he appears to have been responsible for offering the Avro Company at Brooklands a base at Shoreham. Being adjacent to the Adur river they would also be able to test seaplanes. So Avro came to Shoreham, and set up in sheds 3 and 4. Avro's Chief Test Pilot was H.R. Simms, and he was assisted by Howard Pixton, another well known flier of the times.

Avro also built planes at Shoreham for private customers, and in 1912 they built a small single seat plane for a Lt. Burga of the Peruvian Navy. It was fitted with differentially actuated vertical surfaces above and below the fuselage instead of ailerons. However this system was not a success, and the machine was later damaged during a test flight by H.R. Simms.

By this time Avro had also moved their flying school to Shoreham using Avros Type D. Later the prototype Type E and an Avro 500 joined the fleet. One of the instructors was a John Alcock who just six years later would become world famous for his trans-Atlantic crossing in a Vickers Vimy with Arthur Whitten-Brown.

Shoreham now boasted a Pavilion/Clubhouse, a restaurant plus tennis courts, and a croquet lawn! There was also a golf course nearby. Mr. James Funnell was the Groundsman.

## *1913*

In January 1913, the Brighton-Shoreham Aero Club Dinner was held at the Royal York Hotel. The Managing Director G.A. Wingfield outlined the progress made, and recalled the twelve distinguished aviators who had visited Shoreham during its first year of operation.

Another resident at Shoreham about this time was G.M. Dyott who had first obtained his Brevet No. 114 on a Bleriot at Hendon in 1911. The following year he decided to have a plane built to his own design, and he took delivery of his Dyott monoplane powered by a 50 h.p. Gnome engine in 1913. He kept it at Shoreham for a while, and a photo taken in 1913 shows it outside a new hangar which had been built on the eastern boundary. This hangar was given the designation of No. 1, but it may have been destroyed by fire that year as it does not appear in photos taken a year later. Dyott then took his plane to the U.S.A. for a six month tour flying over 2000 miles around the States.

During 1913, the War Office was offered a contract for hangarage at four shillings a day plus landing rights. Despite a fair number of occupants during the year the income was less than expected, and the contract lapsed.

However, about this time the RFC began to show an interest in Shoreham as a possible Squadron base, and a Captain W.D. Beatty made a report on the aerodrome and its facilities. In it he detailed the number of hangars and other buildings, and the extent of the aerodrome at the time. Interestingly he noted that some of the ditches shown on the maps of the time had in fact been filled in, except for a few on the northern boundary.( A copy of his three-page report and map is included in the Appendix.)

In April, Gustav Hamel arrived at Shoreham with the intrepid Miss Trehawke Davies in her new two-seater Bleriot monoplane. They had just been low-flying off Brighton beach, during which the plane is alleged to have actually touched the water! The pair then flew on to Dover en route for Cologne, but at Dover it seems her seat was taken by a journalist who wanted to write an article about the threat of the new German Zeppelins.

Miss Trehawke had already flown across the Channel with Hamel on April 2nd 1912, becoming the first woman to do so.

Early in 1913, Gordon England had reappeared at Shoreham after a period working with Bristols. He had met James Radley who had a new Waterplane project, and the two agreed to produce it jointly, with Radley providing the finance and Gordon England being retained as the designer and pilot.

Initially they took over shed No. 6 vacated by B.H. England, but later a new larger hangar was built in the south-east corner beyond Piffard's original shed. The workers consisted of Foreman Tom Davis (who used to measure wood with a micrometer!), Tom Male, Ern Aylyer and an engineer from Bristol's, Ern Briginshaw. George Lapthorne was the Foreman of the Metal Department, and was assisted by a an elderly blacksmith by the name of Bray who did the tube bending. Charles Gates was retained as the "boy" still on five shillings a week.

In his tape recordings held in the archives of The Shoreham Airport Collection, Charles Gates revealed some interesting facts about working conditions in 1913. A normal working day was from 6 a.m. to 6 p.m., and 6 a.m. to 12 noon on Saturdays. Overtime was frequently worked up to 8 p.m., and workers brought food for three meals (no works canteens in those days). Breakfast time was from 8 a.m. to 8.30 a.m., the mid-day meal was from 12-1, and they stopped around 6 p.m. for the evening meal.

The Radley-England Waterplane, as it became known, had already flown at Portholme aerodrome near Cambridge on a temporary set of wheels. It had a rather unique engine installation designed by Gordon England, with three 50 h.p. Gnome rotary engines mounted in tandem, driving a huge nine foot ten inch diameter propeller! Each of the twin floats had three seats, and the pilot flew the aircraft from the front of the right-hand float.

Charles Gates assisted with the re-erection and subsequent manhandling of the machine over the river bank on a specially graded ramp into the Adur for taxi-ing trials. Later it was towed by motor boat the six miles down to Volk's electric railway station on Brighton beach for flight trials on the open sea. Gordon England made a successful take-off on May 1st 1913, with a reporter as passenger, but was unlucky enough to strike the starboard float on a marker buoy on landing. The float filled with water, and the machine sank in shallow water.

However it was subsequently salvaged, and returned to Shoreham where it underwent a rebuild, emerging with a single 150 h.p. Sunbeam V8 engine, and stronger clinker-built floats which Charles Gates helped to install. In this form it was known as the Waterplane II, and Radley wanted to enter it for the "Daily Mail" Round Britain Race for seaplanes. The young engineer from Sunbeam assisting on the engine installation was John Alcock.

However the Waterplane II was not a success, and would not unstick due to the wrong shape of the floats. Charles Gates considered that was the problem, but Radley chose to blame the new Sunbeam engine, and as a result there was much bitterness, and Alcock departed the scene. He later used the Sunbeam engine in a Farman biplane in which he learnt to fly, and then used it to demonstrate the Sunbeam engine. Thereafter the Waterplane project was abandoned.

In the meantime on May 28th 1913, Avro pilot Frederick Raynham had test flown the first Avro 503 floatplane from the Adur with John Alcock as passenger. The following day Raynham flew it to Paston Place, Brighton, and landed it in the open sea opposite the Volk's Seaplane hangar. Initial trials were most successful, and the type showed great promise.

However one day Raynham suffered engine failure at only fifty feet, just after he took off from the Adur towards the railway bridge. Miraculously he managed to touch down between one of the spans without damage. When the mechanics checked later it was found that he had just nine inches clearance at the wing tips, and only six inches above!

The Avro 503 was eventually sold to the Germans and manufactured under licence. An Avro 504 was also fitted with floats, and tested on the river Adur. However, this plane also suffered engine failure while coming to land from the east, and Raynham crashed into a poultry run on the east bank, demolishing both plane and poultry, but without injury to himself.

Also in May 1913, Eric and Cecil Pashley decided to move their joy-flight business from Brooklands to Shoreham. No doubt they were attracted by cheaper rental, and the potential joyriding business from the large population of the area. Nearby beaches would also provide landing sites. They used a Maurice Farman "Longhorn" for ten minute joy-flights, and they occupied part of the Avro shed. Cecil Pashley was soon involved with the Brighton-Shoreham Aero Club, which he later reconstituted as the Sussex County Aero Club. Thus began the Pashley Brothers' association with Shoreham which was to last a lifetime for Cecil.

At midday on June 17th, a Maurice Farman piloted by Lieutenants Granville and Small left Larkhill for Shoreham, but they lost their way in fog and crashed near Hangleton Church to the north-west of Hove. However both escaped injury.

On June 29th 1913, Shoreham witnessed its first fatal accident. Richard Norman Wight stalled his Avro 500 biplane, and dived into the garden of New Salts Farm to the south of the railway line. The wreckage burst into flames, and although Wight was still alive, his would-be rescuers had difficulty in cutting him free. By the time wire cutters had been found he had received fatal burns, and died the same night in Sussex County Hospital. He had been transported to the hospital by Eric Pashley who was later fined five pounds for speeding! (A harsh penalty under the circumstances as the speed limit at the time was only 20 m.p.h.). The crash was a major blow for the Avro Flying School.

Some people claimed that Wight's real surname was Gair, as many pilots of the time disguised their names to avoid recognition by relatives who did not approve of flying. However the official records still show Wight.

In July, Eric Pashley had his leg broken by a pupil who ran into him on a motor bike, and he was not able to fly for four months. However Cecil continued flying, and it is estimated that by the end of 1913 they had flown over ten thousand miles.

Late in July a large Breguet Biplane was brought over to Shoreham from France piloted by their Chief Test Pilot, Henri Bregi, and accompanied by Mrs. Buller in her Breguet. The same Mrs. Buller was an early passenger of Morison at Shoreham in 1911, and she had learnt to fly herself in France in May 1912 at Douai.

Inbetween events Charles Gates got away from the daily chores, and went to events like the 1913 Olympia Aero Show. There he met and talked to the great Samuel Cody who was to lose his life at Farnborough in August that year. In fact Cody flew high over Shoreham on his way to Farnborough just three days before that sad event.

In 1913 Horatio Barber presented the Royal Aero Club with the Britannia Trophy. It was to be awarded each year to the British aviator with the most meritorious performance in the air.

Awards were made in 1913 and 1914, but then held over during the war. Among the later holders were well-known identities such as Sir John Alcock (posthumous) in 1919, and Bert Hinkler in 1920.

The Avro Flying School left Shoreham in September 1913 after training only three pilots for their Brevets. Probably Wingfield had tried to increase the rent, but also the operation had been none too successful for Avro, and there had been complaints about the poor condition of their aircraft. Their Chief Pilot had already departed earlier in the year after a dispute over the Bruga monoplane.

Frank Raynham also left Shoreham at this stage, and went out to Malaya with the intrepid Tsoe Wong where they ran a service using Avro 504s between Penang and Kuala Lumpur. Although Wong had left Shoreham disgraced, he had great ability, and eventually became well-known in his country in the political sphere.

The Sussex County Aero Club had some well-known identities among its members in 1913. One was C.G. Grey, long-time Editor of the aviation journal "The Aeroplane".

On November 8th 1913, there was yet another air race, this time from Hendon to Brighton and back, and nine competitors took part. Among them were pilots who had featured earlier in the history of Shoreham: Pierre Verrier in a Farman, G.M. Dyott in his Dyott monoplane just back from his tour of the U.S.A., Robert Slack in a Morane Saulnier monoplane, Fred Raynham also in a Morane Saulnier and Gustav Hamel in a 80 h.p. Gnome-Morane Saulnier. The race was full of incidents. For example the pilot of one of the Bleriots decided to return when his compass fell into his lap! Raynham's engine came to a standstill when the wire controlling his carburettor broke over Horley at ten thousand feet resulting in a forced landing. Dyott also made a forced landing near Beachy Head after being blown off course. He was almost successful, but was overturned by a gust of wind, and although unhurt and with little damage to his plane, he had to retire. Pierre Verrier was declared the winner, followed by Hamel, with Slack in fourth place.

After the demise of the Waterplanes, Radley built the unusual annular monoplanes designed by G. Tilghman Richards and his partner, Cedric Lee. Gordon England assisted with some work on the structure and engine installation. He was also employed as test pilot at ten pounds an hour.

A draughtsman by the name of William Boyne was engaged, and the first machine was built in great secrecy in shed No. 7 on large circular jigs.

Gordon England made the first flight on November 23rd 1913. After several preliminary hops he suddenly found himself airborne. So he elected to continue and make the first proper flight. He flew over Lancing and Worthing for about forty-five minutes. However as he was approaching to land the engine suddenly stopped, and he lost control. The aircraft flipped over to the inverted position before rolling right side up, and then pancaked into the telephone wires alongside the railway line.

Gordon England was lucky to survive the accident which kept him on crutches with a damaged knee for several weeks. Trains were delayed as the wreckage blocked the railway line for several hours.

Charles Gates agreed with the findings that the accident was probably due to the centre of gravity being too far aft. The engine had cut out when he apparently ran out of fuel, and when the thrust component was lost, the centre of gravity became critical.

About this time Radley sold the business to Cedric Lee who then brought in an American secretary named Spence, and with him came greater efficiency and job cards etc. But Tilghman Richards who was now in charge of construction found the new secretary too interfering, and there was friction.

Cedric Lee wanted to enter the Annular Monoplane in the Gordon Bennett Air Race to be held in Paris in September 1914, so it was decided to rebuild the first prototype, with modifications to the biplane tail, but nothing seems to have been done about moving the centre of gravity. The test flying program resumed, but according to Charles Gates it was largely numerous "hops", and it is doubtful whether it was ever flown outside the aerodrome again.

One of the interesting claims made by the designers of the annular planes was the better stability due to the vortex effect through the central hole of eleven foot diameter. According to Charles Gates, when the aerodrome was water-logged, a definite spume of water could be seen going up through the hole to some height above it as it taxied at speed.

Gordon England then handed over test flying to Gordon Bell, and a few "hops" were also made by N.S. Percival.

## *1914*

Early in 1914 a new Sopwith 3-seater cabin plane landed at Shoreham, and later Charles Gates watched it take off with a Lt. F.P. Reenie at the controls, only to come down in a Tulip farm (later Easter's field) beyond the western boundary, but without injury to the pilot.

In March 1914 the Pashley Brothers decided to break away from the Shoreham Flying School with whom they had been associated, and set up the Pashley Flying School. They were by now firmly established as flying instructors, and were to go on and train many pilots who later flew with the RFC. A former pupil of the Pashleys named Bernard Hale, who gained his Brevet No. 176 on May 18th 1914, later joined them as an instructor, and for a short while they operated as Pashley Brothers & Hale.

On April 10th 1914, Gordon Bell made the first hop in the second annular monoplane, and then made a number of flights without incident. However a fortnight later disaster struck again. At around eight hundred feet he got into difficulties, and descended in a flat spin. As Charles Gates said, "he came down like a frisbee". The aircraft was a total write-off, but remarkably Bell survived. A later inquiry revealed that one of the elevator eye bolts had come out, jamming the elevators hard down. Fortunately for Bell the cushioning effect of the air fifty feet from the ground had freed the jammed elevator, and it righted itself before pancaking.

Despite this setback construction proceeded with a third model, but with a monoplane tail, and using wooden spars instead of the steel tubes used in the first two machines. Bell claimed this made it too flexible and dangerous to fly.

He demonstrated this machine to Winston Churchill during a visit to Shoreham in June 1914, but the demonstration flight ended in a heavy landing causing damage. Winston had asked to be taken up in one so they were able to put him off. Perhaps it was just as well in view of his later place in history . . .

Bell then told Cedric Lee he would not continue with the test flying, and if he wanted to, he could fly the b . . . . . thing himself!

So Bell departed. Some time later after repairs, Cedric Lee attempted a flight. While he made a successful take-off towards the Adur river, he lost control and pancaked in the river mud without injury, but ending the story of the annular monoplanes.

In May another of Shoreham's early fliers had been lost. Gustav Hamel disappeared over the Straits of Dover on a cross-channel flight on May 23rd 1914. He had been progressively shortening his wings in the quest for speed, and this made his machine very unstable. It is thought he may have simply lost control near the water.

In July 1914 the Pashley Brothers built and flew a biplane of their own design. Similar to a Farman, it had a 50 h.p. Gnome engine, and had seating for two passengers with a top speed of sixty-one m.p.h. However Charles Gates said he thought that Eric Pashley did most of the flying in it, and regarded it as his own personal mount.

Meanwhile the RFC was busy building up its strength as war clouds loomed, and about this time a flight of the new B.E. 2s from No. 6 Squadron landed at Shoreham on a cross-country flight from Farnborough.

Cedric Lee left Shoreham about this time and joined the RNAS, but was later to lose his life during the Gallipoli landings. However the Cedric Lee workforce continued under his Manager William Spence, and later moved to a factory in the Bungalow Town area, where they built Avros for the rest of the war.

Earlier the Cedric Lee Company had won a contract to manufacture BE. 2c wings. With wages earned from this contract, Charles Gates and another carpenter named Fred Wallis started making their own plane using parts from an ancient Bleriot monoplane, and a three cylinder Anzani engine. They built it in a room above a boot-repairer's shop in Southwick, and later in a garage just south of the railway in Southwick.

It resembled a Caudron biplane, and they got as far as making the body, mounting the engine and constructing the wings. However, they were not to complete its construction as Gates would leave Shoreham to join up as a boy mechanic with the RNAS in May 1915. He had wanted to learn to fly, but nobody would take him seriously at Shoreham, so he just went off and volunteered for the RNAS which offered him some hope of learning to fly. In fact it was to be 1916 in far-off Dar-es-Salaam in East Africa before Charles Gates first flew as an air mechanic.

Years later in 1924, Fred Wallis would help a young Fred Miles build his first plane in his father's laundry in Portslade, using components from the partly completed Gates and Wallis plane.

Charles Gates also had another link with Fred Miles. Both were taught at the same school in Portslade, but six years apart, by the same teacher who happened to be Charles Gates' eldest brother. Charles was the youngest of a family of five, being born in 1897.

The Gates and Miles families were to be further entwined in later years when Grahame Gates, son of the teacher, joined Miles Aircraft Ltd. in 1942 at Woodley, and served with them as a weights engineer and aerodynamicist for many years. Later he worked for George Miles at Airspeed's as a stressman, before fate eventually brought him to Shoreham with F.G. Miles Ltd. in 1951, and history repeated itself with another generation of the Gates family working at Shoreham!

The Gates family also have a link with nearby Lancing College Chapel which has long featured in the background at Shoreham Airport. Grahame Gates's father, Mr. Arthur Gates, besides being a teacher, was also an accomplished woodcarver, and he carved the donors' names on some 200 pews in the Chapel which are still in use today.

Charles Gates served with No. 7 Squadron in East Africa, but was sent back to the U.K. after a bout of malaria. He was eventually transferred to the RAF, trained as an Observer at Eastchurch in 1918, and was finally commissioned on September 20th 1918. He took part in early experiments with air radio, and was in the RAF attempt on a trans-Atlantic flight, but they were beaten by the Americans who flew the Atlantic in stages via the Azores in their Navy flying boats, a short while before the Alcock and Whitten-Brown crossing in 1919.

He went on to a career in Australia joining the RAAF and rose to the rank of Wing Commander. He became the Director of Radio Signals before retiring in 1946. Later he was well known in senior positions of the Department of Reconstruction and Supply as a Radio Engineer. He died in Queensland, Australia on June 6th 1991 at the age of ninety-four. He had never returned to England, but he did meet his nephew Grahame Gates in Australia, and they corresponded right up to his death.

In the weekend flying meetings organised by Wingfield in July 1914 both loops and pylon races entertained the crowd. Winners in the pylon races on July 11th were the Pashley Brothers in their new biplane which they had only completed a few days before. A photograph of the event shows both horse-drawn carriages and early motor vehicles in the spectators' enclosure. John Alcock, or "Jack" as he was called in the reports of the time, took part in the races in his Sunbeam-engined Farman.

Grahame-White's Farman seaplane "WakeUp England" in which he raced
against a motor launch off Brighton on July 24th 1911.
Photo: "Aeroplane Monthly" Sept. 1979.

The Martin Handasyde in which Graham Gilmour lost his life when the left wing
broke off in turbulent conditions on February 17th 1912.
Photo: "Flight".

The first photo of the Pashley brothers at Shoreham taken in 1912.
Photo: Miles Aircraft Ltd./Adwest Archives.

The Chanter Flying School at Shoreham before the disastrous fire of February 1912. Seen
here are the school's two Bleriot XI's and the Chanter Nieuport monoplane.
Photo: "Aeroplane Monthly" Sept. 1979.

Pierre Verrier seen here at Shoreham in 1912 in his 70 h.p. Maurice Farman "Longhorn".
Photo: The Shoreham Airport Collection.

A Wong two-seat Biplane similar to the "Wong Mei" which was
being built at Shoreham in 1912.
Photo: JMB/GSL Collection

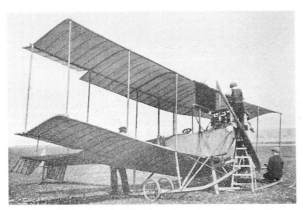

The modified Collyer-England Biplane with a larger 35 h.p. Green engine
and an altered undercarriage. This was the machine which Wong crashed.
Photo: C.F. Andrews.

The Burga monoplane at Shoreham in November 1912. The unusual feature of lateral control rudders above and below the fuselage can be seen in this view.
Photo: British Aircraft 1809-1914.

The Radley-Moorhouse Bleriot racing monoplane seen here at Shoreham in 1913. (Sharp-eyed readers will be able to see the nose of an annular monoplane just behind the rudder of the Bleriot.)
Photo: Royal Aero Club.

# WELL-KNOWN EARLY FLIERS AT SHOREHAM IN 1912

L. to R.: G. Hamel, R.T. Gates,* W.L Brock, R.B. Slack.
*General Manager, Hendon aerodrome (not related to Chas. Gates)
Photo: The Shoreham Airport Collection.

Gustav Hamel on the right with his 80 h.p. Morane Saulnier.
Photo: The Shoreham Airport Collection.

R.B. Slack at Shoreham with his 80 h.p. Morane Saulnier.
Photo: "Aeroplane Monthly" Sept. 1979.

The Dyott monoplane outside the "No.1 hangar" built on the eastern boundary around 1913.
However it does not appear to have lasted long as there is no sign of it in the photo below
taken a year later. The little gatehouse which can be seen over the left wing also appears in
the photo of the weekend Flying Meeting in July 1914, but again the hangar has gone.
Photo: The Shoreham Airport Collection.

A signed photo of G.M. Dyott standing beside his machine at Shoreham in 1914.
Photo: JMB/GSL Collection.

MISS TREHAWKE DAVIES.

Miss Trehawke Davies handing Mr. Gustav Hamel his goggles prior to ascending with Mr. Hamel in his monoplane at Hendon on Friday, January 2nd, for the purpose of looping the loop, Miss Davies being the first woman to go through this remarkable experience in Great Britain.

These photographs are reproduced from the "Flight" magazine of January 10th 1914.

The Radley-England Waterplane I on a temporary wheel
undercarriage at Portholme aerodrome.
Photo: "Flight".

The power plant for the Radley-England Waterplane I designed by Gordon England.
It had three 50 h.p. Gnome engines coupled to a common shaft by chain drives
(synchronising them would have been tricky!).
Photo: Gordon England.

The Radley England Waterplane I off the south coast in 1913.
Photo: Gordon England.

The Radley-England Waterplane II seen here on the River Adur. Note the large radiator for the Sunbeam engine just below the leading edge of the top wing.
Photo: JMB/GSL Collection.

The Avro 503 floatplane seen here on the beach at Shoreham.
Photo: "Aeroplane Monthly" Sept. 1979.

Gordon England

Frederick Raynham

Members of the Avro Flying School with the Avro Type D.
Photo: JMB/GSL Collection.

The Pashley brothers pose with their Farman at Shoreham in 1913.
Cecil on the left, Eric on the right.
Photo: JMB/GSL Collection.

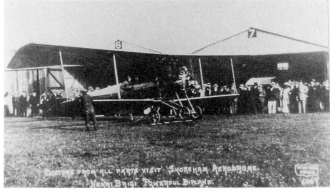

Henri Bregi's massive Biplane at Shoreham being inspected by a group of doctors at a
conference in 1913.
Photo: The Shoreham Airport Collection.

Farman seaplane on the Adur at Shoreham around 1913.
Photo: "Aeroplane Monthly" Sept. 1979.

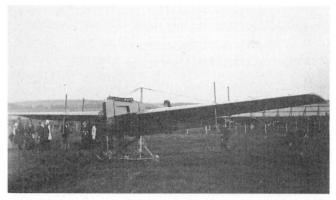

This Martinsyde monoplane fitted with a 120 h.p. Austro Daimler
motor was in the London to Brighton race on November 8th 1913.
Photo: JMB/GSL Collection.

Eric Pashley with a passenger in their Henry Farman Biplane
at Shoreham on June 16th 1914.
Photo: "Aeroplane Monthly".

The prototype Lee-Richards Annular Monoplane seen here at Shoreham before its first
flight on November 23rd 1913. The tail-down attitude suggests a "tail-dragger", but the
photo below clearly shows it had a tricycle undercarriage. It is thought that the plane was
tipped into this position to reveal the circular wing format.
Photo: "Flight".

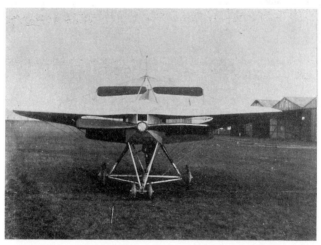

This view shows the sturdy undercarriage and the upper section of the biplane tail.
Photo: The Shoreham Airport Collection.

## THE CEDRIC LEE MONOPLANE.

As in the early days of the Dunne machine, considerable mystery enshrouds the Cedric Lee monoplane, practical experiments with which have been carried out at the Shoreham aerodrome for some months past. Not the least point of interest in connection with the Cedric Lee monoplane is that it is more or less at variance with certain aerodynamical theories as accepted to-day. Unfortunately, detailed particulars of this interesting machine cannot at present be placed before our readers, as the Cedric Lee Co. do not yet wish these to be made public. Since, however, several successful flights have been made in public, and as entries have been made for the coming Gordon-Bennett race, the following brief particulars, together with the accompanying illustrations, should be of special interest. The most important feature of this machine is that it flies "pterygoid," that is, like a dart, or its length is greater than its span. The latter, in fact, is only some 20 ft. The planes are annular in plan form, being centrally divided fore and aft by the *fuselage*. The whole of the plane section in side elevation forms one large camber, but the front portion of the plane is also cambered. The covered-in *fuselage* is rectangular in section, tapering to a vertical knife-edge at the rear. In the middle of the *fuselage*, in the "hole" of the plane, are the passenger's and pilot's seats, the former occupying the front one, where an excellent view below can be obtained. The engine, a 50 h.p. Gnome, which drives a tractor screw, is placed inside the *fuselage* in front of the passenger's seat, air scoops being fitted in the sides of the *fuselage* for cooling. Hinged to the rear extremity of the plane are two elevators, whilst two others are mounted above them, one on each side of the vertical rudder, which is hinged to the rear end of the *fuselage* and to a vertical fin mounted on to top of the latter. A strong three-wheeled chassis is fitted, one wheel being right in front to protect the propeller. It is claimed that this particular model has a speed range of from 45 m.p.h. to well over 70 m.p.h. Strong construction is another of its features; on one occasion a landing was made on one of the "wing tips,"

but the machine only rolled a little way on the outer edge of the plane and then settled down on its chassis

The Cedric Lee machine in flight.

again without any ill effects. Mr. Gordon England has made several flights on this machine, and just recently Gordon Bell has joined the Cedric Lee Co., and has also made several flights. Unfortunately he met last week-end with one of those accidents that must always be associated with valuable experimental work, so that activities will be delayed for the present, but we understand that the two machines for the Gordon-Bennett are well in hand at the works.

A fine study of Cecil Pashley flying with a passenger at Shoreham in 1914. The machine is a
Maurice Farman MF 7 "Longhorn" which was a popular basic trainer of the time, and many
RFC pilots had their first flight in them. It was powered by a 70 h.p. Renault V-8 engine,
and it had a maximum speed of about 59 m.p.h. (95 km/hr).
Photo: "Flight" January 10th 1914.

The Pashley Biplane built in 1914, outside the Sussex County Aero Club. The six-cylinder
"Prince Henry" Austro Daimler in the foreground was owned by Cedric Lee.
Photo: "Aeroplane Monthly" Sept. 1979.

Charles Gates as an RAF Officer around
1918. Note his Observer's badge.

Photo: Grahame Gates.

The Gates-Wallis project in storage
during WW I. The three cylinder Anzani
engine and the partly built wing units are
visible.

Photo: Grahame Gates.

# FLYING AT SHOREHAM.

ALREADY the new management of the Brighton-Shoreham aerodrome have found time to effect quite a number of improvements in the arrangements at the ground, and the weekly flying meetings which are to be held during the present season should make this aerodrome very popular indeed. The ground itself is particularly adapted for the purpose, as it is absolutely level and as smooth as a lawn. The course itself, which is marked off by pylons, is a little over 1¾ miles long, and the last pylon before the home straight is so situated that in speed races round the pylons the competitors bank very steeply in fairly close proximity to the enclosures, so that an excellent view of the various ways in which the different pilots handle their machines can be obtained. Several new sheds have been erected to accommodate visitors' machines. In addition to the excellent flying, other attractions provided include well-appointed tennis courts and tea gardens, and on race days a military band provides a very good programme of music. The headquarters of the Sussex County Aero Club are situated on the flying ground adjoining the hangars. For the opening meeting of the season which took place on Saturday last the management were fortunate in having favourable weather conditions. That the efforts to improve the aerodrome are appreciated was shown by the large crowd which arrived from various parts of the country by road or rail, and it must be recorded that the meeting was exceedingly well organised. The officials were : Directors, Messrs. G. Arthur Wingfield (chairman), H. V. Fabrin, H. Wingfield, W. Pettett ; General Manager, Mr. John Bellham ; Secretary, Mr. W. C. Littlewood ; Aerodrome Manager, Capt. C. A. Tyrer, L.F. ; Judges, Mr. W. B. Gentle and Mr. R. Brodrick ; Clerk of the Course, Mr. H. Gonne ; Stewards, Col. Hudson, Col. A. Woolley, J.P., and Messrs. J. T. Musgrave, T. Blair, G. T. Richards and O. Mellersh.

Among the pilots who were flying on Saturday may be mentioned J. L. Hall, Eric and Cecil Pashley, J. Alcock, W. H. Elliott and G. J. Lusted. Jack Alcock flew across from Brooklands on Saturday morning accompanied by a passenger, in his 100 h.p. Sunbeam-engined Maurice Farman biplane, completing the journey in 38 mins. J. L. Hall had arrived from Brooklands the previous evening on his Avro biplane. The proceedings of the day commenced with test flights by Hall on his Avro, Alcock on the M. Farman, and E. Pashley on a new small biplane of the pusher type, built by the Pashley brothers. This machine, although following standard lines in its general arrangement, is an extremely neat job, and the Pashley brothers are to be congratulated on their skill as constructors as well as pilots. The machine has been built quite recently, in fact it was only erected on the previous Sunday, and it was Thursday before the engine was fitted, and it may be mentioned that the Pashleys did most of the constructional work themselves.

At four o'clock Mr. Hall got into his machine, and starting off with a very steep climb soon climbed to about 2,200 ft. Having reached this height, Mr. Hall put the nose of his Avro biplane downwards and made a vertical dive of several hundred feet, to gain speed, and then pulling back his elevator, he made one of the cleanest loops we have seen, afterwards landing with a beautiful spiral *vol plané*. Shortly after the speed race was started, this race including two heats of four laps each and a final of six laps, the prizes being the Brighton Cup, and cash prizes aggregating £100, presented by the proprietors of "Shell" motor spirit.

In the first heat Cecil Pashley on an old-type Henry Farman biplane, received a start of 3 mins. from Jack Alcock who was flying his M. Farman. Competing unofficially was W. H. Elliott, also on an old-type Henry Farman biplane. Although banking his machine round the pylons at alarming angles, Alcock did not succeed in beating Cecil Pashley, who won by 31¾ secs. In the second heat, J. L. Hall was scratch on his Avro biplane, whilst Eric Pashley on the new Pashley biplane received 1 min. start. Competing unofficially was G. J. Lusted on a Henry Farman biplane by 1 min. 3¾ secs. This heat was won easily by Eric Pashley by 1 min. 3¾ secs.

Four machines were entered in the final : (1) Eric Pashley on Pashley biplane (2 mins. 25 secs. start) ; (2) J. L. Hall, Avro biplane (30 secs. start) ; (3) J. Alcock, M. Farman biplane (scratch). Cecil Pashley on one of the Farmans competed unofficially and received 3 mins. 45 secs. start. All the pilots handled their machines in excellent style, but although Hall's and Alcock's experience at Brooklands and Hendon stood them in good stead, they did not succeed in beating Eric Pashley, who won by 39¾ secs. There appeared to be very little difference between the speed of the Avro and that of the M. Farman, as Alcock finished 27 secs. behind Hall, whose handicap allowance was 30 secs. Eric Pashley's fine win was greeted with enthusiasm by the spectators, amongst whom the Pashley brothers are evidently very popular, and he thus secured the Brighton Cup and £70, whilst Hall, who was second man home, received £20 and Alcock £10.

On Sunday the heavy rain in the morning was followed by a very fine afternoon, during which numerous exhibition and passenger flights were given. J. L. Hall and Eric Pashley had another try round the pylons under the same handicap conditions as those in the race on Saturday, but whereas in the Saturday's race Pashley won by 39¾ secs., he only managed on Sunday to get home 8 secs. ahead of Hall.

In the evening, in the presence of a good number of spectators, Mr. Hall went up again and repeated his performance of looping the loop.

"Machines lined up for the start of the second heat of the speed race at the Shoreham aerodrome. From left to right: John Alcock's Farman, The Pashley brothers' Biplane, Hall's Avro 500".

The spectators' enclosure at the weekly Flying Meeting held on July 14th 1914. Note that the little gatehouse is also in this view, and the rear of the Waterplane hangar is on the extreme right.
Photo: "Flight" July 17th 1914.

"Cecil Pashley banking one of the Farmans round a pylon at last Saturday's speed race at the Shoreham aerodrome". This view clearly shows the location of buildings of the period.
Photo: "Flight" July 14th 1914.

"A fine bank by J. Alcock."

"An old aeroplane wing makes an excellent awning in the Sussex Aero Club's enclosure".

# Chapter 2　WORLD WAR I AND THE CANADIANS (1914–1921)

On August 4th 1914 war with Germany was declared, and the days of air races and fun flying came to a end. However, unlike the second world war, there was no immediate threat of air attacks, and a few private fliers under training with Pashley Bros. and Hale continued with their flying. Before closing their Flying School in December 1914, Pashley Bros. and Hale issued a further ten Brevets. The Pashleys then left Shoreham, but their Pashley biplane remained on site in one of the hangars for some time. Its eventual fate is not known.

Eric Pashley test flew with Vickers, and then joined the RFC in 1916. He was with No. 24 Squadron based at Bertangles near Arras, and was accredited with shooting down eight enemy aircraft, and forcing down two others. That should have rated him as an ace, but no official recognition was ever made. Sadly he was to lose his life, not at enemy hands, but through a flying accident on March 17thΔ 1917, while on active service.

Cecil on the other hand went as a Flying Instructor to the Seaplane School of the Northern Aircraft Company, and taught flying off Lake Windermere. Then in the autumn of 1915, he joined the Grahame-White Flying School at Hendon training many hundreds of pilots for the RFC.

For a short while the aerodrome was inactive and deserted. This attracted the attention of a young R. Dallas Brett, then a schoolboy at Lancing College. He and two companions abandoned their train-spotting excursion, and squeezed under the aerodrome fence. Through cracks in the wooden hangar walls they saw the Pashley biplane and some of the Farmans. In another hangar they found the Dyott monoplane.

Then Major Gerrard of the Royal Marines requisitioned the aerodrome for the Government, and took over all the planes. Wingfield had all his assets taken, and was engaged in lengthy proceedings against the Government which ended up with appeals to the House of Lords, and which nearly bankrupted him.

## *1915*

On January 15th 1915 the RFC formally took over Shoreham, and established No. 3 Reserve Squadron (for basics of flying). One of Shoreham's early fliers, Horatio Barber was among the first instructors, and he was reputed to have had such a loud voice he could be heard from the ground shouting instructions in the air to his pupils! The Squadron was equipped with Maurice Farman Longhorns and Shorthorns (known as "Rumpetys"), F.E. 2ds and Avro 504Ks.

While Wingfield battled for compensation, the flying training continued, and some famous names were among the ninety-seven Brevets issued at Shoreham in 1915. Among them was Sir Sholto Douglas, who was to become an Air Chief Marshal and AOC-in-C Fighter Command in 1940, taking over from Sir Hugh Dowding.

No. 14 Squadron was formed at Shoreham on February 3rd 1915, but its members were largely drawn from No. 3 Reserve Squadron. They used Farmans and Martinsydes to gradually work up the Squadron which took them many months, but by November they were deemed fit for active service. They left behind their Farmans and Martinsydes, and went out to Egypt where they joined forces with No. 17 Squadron flying the new B.E. 2cs. No. 14 Squadron served in the Middle East campaigns in the Western Desert, the Suez Canal and the Sinai Peninsula.

Thereafter No. 14 served in Palestine, and had its part in the famous rout of the Turks at Wadi el Far'a in September 1918. At that stage they were flying the Martinsyde Elephants. No. 14 Squadron was disbanded at Tangmere on February 4th 1919, but was to be revived later and went on to serve in WW II. Once again they served in the Middle East flying Blenheim Mk. 4s and Marauders. No. 14 returned to the U.K. in 1944 to fly Wellington GR Mk XIVs from Chivenor in Devon.

On February 4th 1915, a Canadian airman under training, Lt. William Sharpe, was killed when his Maurice Farman side-slipped and dived into a field between the Sussex Pad and Lancing College. This crash was described by Charles Gates in his tapes, and caused the Head Master at Lancing College to put the aerodrome out of bounds. However that did not stop generations of boys from following events at Shoreham. Indeed many had their first interest in aviation kindled by its very presence.

Many ex-pupils, like Stanley F. Vincent, enjoyed returning to their former seat of learning, and to do aerobatics over the College. In 1915 he performed in his B.E.2c at the end of a cross country flight to Shoreham while under training with the RFC at Beaulieu.

Despite the aerodrome being out of bounds, it was irresistible to Dallas Brett and his friends, and during the early part of 1915 they were caught emerging from the aerodrome on three occasions! Each time they were beaten with increasing severity by their House Master, Adam Fox.

However, a little later the Commanding Officer invited the Head Master to visit the aerodrome, and took him on a flight which he enjoyed. As a direct result, organised tours were arranged to the aerodrome, and of course Dallas Brett and his friends were on the first tour. However they were highly embarrassed when an instructor greeted them with the words "Hello you three, here again!" Despite this awkward moment, all was forgiven and Dallas Brett was taken up in a Farman as far as Hove Lawns and back. Over Bungalow Town the pilot executed tight turns over some girls waving from a garden which caused him a moment of anxiety! Inspired by this flight Dallas Brett eventually went into the aviation industry at Brooklands working for Sopwiths.

## *1916*

Wingfield continued his battle, and after a High Court case was found against him he went to the Court of Appeal, and the House of Lords. He finally won compensation for £25,000, and was able to settle his debts.

Another famous name appeared on the list of trainees at Shoreham in 1916. He was Harold Balfour, later Member of Parliament and Under Secretary of State for Air in 1938.

The first man to fly from England to Ireland in 1910 was Bob Lorraine, and he also trained as a RFC pilot at Shoreham in 1916. As an Observer, Lorraine had been badly wounded in the early part of the war, taking some months to recover. Later he took a squadron of F.E.8 pusher planes to France.

No. 21 Reserve Squadron was reported as being resident at Shoreham in May 1916. They had been formed at Netheravon in the same month, and it seems probable that they had a detachment "working up" at Shoreham. They then went over to France flying R.E.7s. Other Squadrons were also in residence for short periods, like No. 53 Squadron which was at Shoreham in 1916 with a detachment of four B.E.2cs.

The RFC had to build additional hangars at Shoreham, and these were erected to the west of the original sheds built by Wingfield. At least another eight were added which included three large hangars each 120 feet by 50 feet, situated almost directly behind the site of the hangars built in 1935. From an aerial photo taken about 1919, it would appear the RFC erected other buildings over the tennis courts to the east of No. 3 shed, probably for Squadron administration.

Trainee pilots were to witness a crash highlighting the golden rule of never turning back in the event of engine failure. Lt. Frank Gooden took off from Shoreham with a passenger in a brand - new B.E.2c, and attempted to turn back when the engine failed. He very nearly made it, but stalled over the hangar roofs, and plunged to earth. While he escaped from the burning wreckage his passenger did not.

Another of the boys from Lancing College, Christopher Clarkson, who spent much of his time in and around the aerodrome in the more relaxed climate, managed to hitch a lift in a D.H. 4 on a delivery flight to the Western Front. He got as far as Calais, but was then very promptly returned!

A bit later Clarkson was again in strife with the authorities when he broke bounds with a companion at 10 p.m. They had walked over to the aerodrome where a dance was being held, but it was 2 a.m. before they returned, and of course next day the story got out. They were birched by the Head Master, and also threatened with expulsion.

Although forbidden to go near the aerodrome again, Clarkson was not deterred from his interest in aviation and eventually joined the RAF in 1924. He took a short service commission, and soon showed an exceptional aptitude for flying. After two years with 58 Squadron, then under the command of "Bomber" Harris, he went to the Central Flying School at Upavon as an instructor.

After leaving the RAF in 1929, Clarkson made a name for himself as a stunt pilot at air shows, while working as a development pilot for Airwork. He also wrote flying reports under the pseudonym "Pontius". WW II saw him back in the RAF, and his skills landed him a job with the British Air Commission in New York. He spent much of the war testing new American aircraft like the P.51 Mustang which were of interest to the RAF. He also tested many captured German aircraft like the Me 109 and the FW 190. For this work he was awarded the Air Force Cross. He was appointed Civil Air Attache in Washington in 1948, and on his retirement in 1952, went on to represent large corporations like Vickers Armstrong and the British Aircraft Corporation in the U.S.A. He married three times, and died in June 1994 having attained the ripe old age of 92.

## 1917

Early in 1917 No. 3 Reserve Squadron was renamed No. 3 Training Squadron, which more aptly described its function, and a six week basic flying course began in May using Avro 504Ks. However the minimum of three hours dual followed by only three hours solo was a recipe for disaster. As a result there was a rash of fatal accidents.

On August 21st Lt. W.T. Harris stalled while attempting a forced landing after engine failure, and dived to the ground at Ecclesden Farm near Angmering and died shortly after. Lt. T.C. Kinkhead was killed at Ham Bridge, Worthing following engine failure on September 3rd. Just one day later, Lt. A.A. Leger (French-Canadian) was killed in a crash into the sea when his exhaust manifold fouled the propeller on September 4th. There was yet another crash on September 6th when Lt. V.S. Edmunds was killed after he side-slipped and dived to the ground. All four were buried in the Old Shoreham Cemetery next to St. Nicolas Church.

Early in September 1917, a cadre of 86 Squadron was at Shoreham for a short time after the Squadron was formed at Wye. However, it was constantly drained of personnel to replace losses on the Western Front, and it was disbanded again in July 1918. It was finally reformed in October 1918 flying Sopwith Salamanders.

## 1918

Early in 1918, Stanley Vincent, now a Flight Commander, was sent to Shoreham to form a special Instructors' Flight. This was known as the S.E. Area Flying Instructors' School (SEAFIS). The unit had nineteen Avro 504s, and two of each fighter type then in Squadron service. The course was of fourteen days duration.

About this time there was there was a most extraordinary incident at Shoreham involving an Avro 504K. It was the practice for mechanics to lie across the tailplane to keep it down while the pilot warmed up the engine. However it seems on this occasion the pilot had just landed, and considered a warm- up unnecessary. He took off again straight away with the unfortunate mechanic clinging on for dear life! With the machine very tail-heavy the pilot somehow managed to circle the aerodrome, and coming in over the Adur river induced a flat spin into the soft mud which was fortunately exposed at low tide. The mechanic survived with a broken leg, and the pilot broke his nose on the instrument panel.

(A carbon copy of this incident occurred in WW II when LACW Margaret Horton was accidentally carried aloft by a Spitfire in similar circumstances at RAF Hibaldstow in 1945. She survived unhurt, and the Spitfire Vb involved (AB 910) still flies today with the Battle of Britain Memorial Flight).

A young Don L. Brown, then a schoolboy, witnessed the 1918 incident while on a special pass to the aerodrome granted by the C.O. (In later years the same Don Brown was to become a well-known identity in the Miles Aircraft team, and author of "Miles Aircraft Since 1925").

Don Brown also witnessed a collision over Hove about this time. Four military aircraft were flying west in formation, when two collided. As they did not carry parachutes in those days there were no survivors.

In October 1918, No. 94 Squadron completed its work-up on S.E.5As at Shoreham before going to France.

However on November 11th 1918 the war ended, and so the need for flying training at Shoreham for military needs began to wind down.

## *1919*

Early in 1919 many captured German planes were flown back to Shoreham to show staff. S.F. Vincent flew over a Fokker D VII, but approaching Brighton he suffered engine failure, and made a forced landing on the East Brighton Golf Course near Roedean Girls' School (it is interesting to note how many of the early fliers found themselves landing near this particular school!). The girls rushed to the scene, but when they saw the black German crosses they screamed and beat a hasty retreat! However Vincent found he had only run out of petrol, and after refuelling continued his journey to Shoreham where he gave a brilliant display of aerobatics on arrival.

In February 1919 No. 82 Squadron arrived at Shoreham for demobilisation with their B.E. 2cs and Armstrong Whitworth F.K.3s.

It was not long after this that the Flying Instructors' School at Shoreham was closed, and for a while all was quiet.

Then in April 1919 No. 1 Wing of the Canadian Air Force moved from Upper Heyford to Shoreham under their C.O., Capt. A.E. McKeever. The Canadian Wing consisted of No. 1 Squadron with their S.E. 5As, and No. 2 Squadron with D.H. 9A Bombers. No. 1 Squadron had in fact been formed as No. 81 RFC Squadron at Gosport in 1917 as a training squadron. However on November 20th 1918, it was given the role of a fighter unit, and became No. 1 Squadron, Canadian Air Force, probably because it had a heavy content of Canadians.

No. 82 Squadron made way for the Canadians, and went to Tangmere to complete their demobilisation.

There were still many ex-German Fokkers and Rumplers at Shoreham, and as peacetime operations left little to do, the Canadians often used them for aerobatics. On May 22nd 1919, Major Carter, C.O. of No. 2 Squadron, took off to do some aerobatics in a Fokker D VII, but at seven thousand feet over Lancing College the top wing folded up and the machine dived to the ground in the sixteen-acre field just below the College, killing Major Carter instantly. The crash was witnessed by Christopher Clarkson, still a boy at Lancing, who described how the top wing floated down separately long after the main impact. It was the most spectacular crash he saw at Shoreham. Major Carter was buried at the Old Shoreham cemetery along with the other Shoreham fliers killed in 1917.

The activities at Shoreham after this crash were naturally subdued. An ex-RNAS pilot , Lt. Colonel R. Leckie, commanded No. 1 Squadron at this time, and they continued to fly their S.E. 5As while No. 2 plodded round in their war-weary D.H. 9As, badly shaken by the loss of their C.O. A bit later No. 1 Squadron was re-equipped with Sopwith Dolphins, and it is surprising they did not go to No. 2 Squadron to boost their morale.

However financial restraints by the Canadian Government heralded the closure of the Wing at Shoreham later that year, and there was a gradual wind-down. Thus came to an end a period of very intense activity at Shoreham.

For a while in October 1919 there was a fleet of aircraft known as the "Avro Air Fleet" providing joy-flights at West Blatchington Farm near Hove. One of the aircraft in the fleet was an

Armstrong Whitworth F.K.3 (ex RFC/RAF B 9629), and it was seen at Shoreham also showing the civil registration letters G-EABY which were required under new regulations from April 1918 onwards. It would seem Shoreham was used as a maintenance base for the fleet.

Another Shoreham visitor at that time was Bert Hinkler in his Avro Baby G-EACQ, fitted with a 35 h.p. Green engine.

John Alcock, who had figured so much in pre-WW I Shoreham, lost his life on December 18 1919, when he crashed his Vickers Amphibian G-EAOV while attempting a forced landing in fog in Northern France.

Towards the end of 1919, G.A. Wingfield still had one lease from the farmer at New Salts Farm, but it was on a small field on the southern side of the railway known as "Easter's Field". Wingfield tried unsuccessfully to revive the Sussex County Aero Club at this site, but there was little support for the scheme in the post-war climate. He got as far as buying the barn as well as a residence next door to the farm. He even had "Sussex Aero Club" painted on the barn roof, all to no avail . . . (See Historical map, location 2).

## *1920-21*

The Canadians finally disbanded their No. 1 Squadron at Shoreham on January 28th 1920, followed by the Wing H.Q. and No. 2 Squadron on February 5th. Although all flying ceased from then on, the Packing Section remained on site for quite some time clearing up. This apparently included removal of all the wooden hangars, probably because the Government no longer wished to retain the aerodrome, and wanted to hand it back to the farmer clear of everything.

Just who did what during this period is not clear as the Army Camp at Slonk Hill was also advertising in the local papers at the time. They gave details of surplus equipment for sale at the aerodrome which you had to dismantle and collect yourself.

Also there were no less than 65 captured German aircraft which had been brought to Shoreham after the war, and these were gifted to the Canadian Government by the British. Crating all these for shipment took some time, and it was December 1921 before the Packing Section finally completed their work and left Shoreham.

Apparently there was an attempt to sell the aerodrome freehold of 147½ acres, as it was advertised in the "Sussex Daily News" of December 7 1921, but there were no bidders at the auction and it was withdrawn.

The aerodrome then reverted to grazing land, and it would be 1925 before flying returned to Shoreham, but then on the south side of the railway. The original aerodrome would remain as grazing land for the next thirteen years.

**END OF PART 1**

# WORLD WAR I

A Martinsyde Elephant of No. 14 Squadron.

A B.E. 2c as used by No. 14 Squadron in the Middle East.

Squadron photo taken outside the former Sussex County Aero Club premises.
Photo: Ashley Roote.

An aerial view of Shoreham aerodrome taken from the south around 1919.
Photo: "Aeroplane Monthly" December 1979 ("Schoolboy Memories," R. Dallas Brett
OBE).

This is the only known photo of the aerodome as it was in 1919, and Piffard's original shed is still on site (readily identified by its steep pitch roof) right opposite the end of the railway bridge. The first sheds built by Wingfield extend to the west up to where the ditch emerges from under the railway. Beyond that point the additional hangars built for the RFC can be seen up to the edge of the photo. The light and dark patches on the landing ground are probably grass cutting activities, and the white lines reveal the position of filled-in ditches. The Upper Brighton road of the period runs along the northern boundary, crossing the River Adur via the old toll bridge to the right.

Members of C Flight, SEAFIS, with their Avro 504Ks at Shoreham
in 1918. Note the identifying stripes used on the noses.
Photo: JMB/GSL Collection.

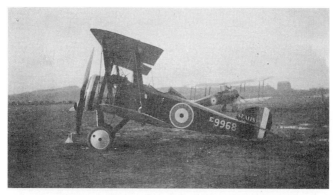

A two-seat Sopwith Camel of SEAFIS and an Avro 504K at Shoreham
in 1918, with Lancing College Chapel in the background.
Photo: JMB/GSL Collection.

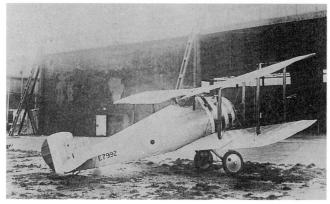

A Sopwith Snipe outside the main hangars in 1918.
Photo: JMB/GSL Collection.

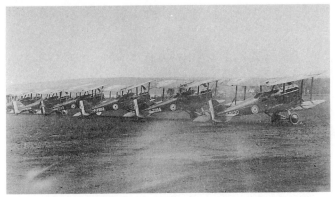

S.E.5as of No. 1 Squadron, Canadian Air Force, at Shoreham in 1919.
Photo: JMB/GSL Collection.

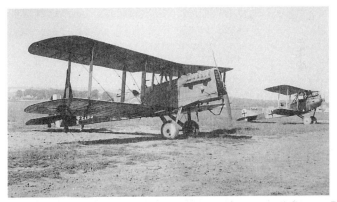

A D.H. 9A of No. 2 Squadron, Canadian Air Force, and a captured German Rumpler
9949/18 in the background.
Photo: JMB/GSL Collection.

Major Carter, DSO, MC, Commander of No. 2 Squadron, Canadian Air Force, with some of
his Officers at Shoreham in 1919.
Photo: JMB/GSL Collection.

Captain A.E. McKeever, C.O. of No. 1 Wing, Canadian Air Force, sitting in the cockpit of a captured German Fokker D.VII at Shoreham in April 1918.
Photo: JMB/GSL Collection.

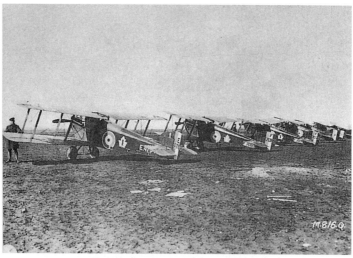

Sopwith Dolphins of No. 1 Squadron, Canadian Air Force, at Shoreham in 1919.
Photo: "Flypast" April 1995.

The Armstrong Whitworth FK 3, G-EABY (ex B9629) which visited Shoreham as part of the Avro fleet in 1919. Seen here at Filton before the application of civil markings.
Photo: "Aeroplane Monthly" Sept. 1979.

The Avro Baby G-EACQ, owned by Bert Hinkler which also visited Shoreham in October 1919. This aircraft still exists at Bundaberg in Queensland, Australia.
Photo: "Aeroplane Monthly" Sept. 1979.

# Part 2 (1922–1939)

## Chapter 3    GNAT AERO AND SOUTHERN AIRCRAFT (1922–1934)

### 1922–1924

This period is the only gap in the continuity of the long and interesting history of Shoreham Airport. While the Canadians and others were busy completing the dismantling of the former RFC hangars etc. during 1921, survivors of the war who had been at Shoreham from its beginnings were about. One in particular was Cecil Pashley who had by then amassed the amazing total of over six thousand hours instructing pilots in the war years. For a while he worked for the Central Aircraft Company in Kilburn, and in 1921 he bought a war surplus Avro 504K which he kept at Hendon. In his spare time he did a little joyriding for the patrons of the Three Frogs Inn at Wokingham up to early 1925.

Meanwhile down in Portslade near Shoreham a young Fred Miles was busy building his first biplane in his father's Star Model Laundry. Born on February 22nd 1903, Fred Miles was the eldest of four sons, and George was the youngest.

Much of this chapter is based on Don L. Brown's book "Miles Aircraft Since 1925", and his later articles "Wings Over Sussex" which were published in the "Aeroplane Monthly" in September and October 1979. Some details have been adjusted following later research.

The war years had been hard on the Miles family and the need to earn money was paramount. Leaving school early, Fred Miles (who was called "Miles" or simply "FG" to those around him) soon demonstrated his independent streak, and began his business career hiring out a rather decrepit motor cycle to the lads of the village for sixpence a time! From that venture he went on to a delivery van service for local businesses using an ancient 23 h.p. Model T Ford van. In this he succeeded quite well until the van expired at the roadside beyond repair. Later he had a job as a projectionist at the Majestic cinema in Kemp Town, Brighton.

Then in 1921 something happened which was to change the direction of his career. At that time Miles had a partly-built sports car which he wanted to sell. It will be recalled from Part 1 that Charles Gates and Fred Wallis had partly-completed a biplane during WW I. However after the war Charles Gates was unable to continue with the project, and so he came to Portslade in the autumn of 1921 to finalise things with Fred Wallis. A meeting was held at the rear of a bicycle shop owned by a man named Deering on Old Shoreham Road, at Southern Cross in Portslade. Fred Miles was present, and a deal was made to swap the partly built-sports car for the partly-built plane! It is not clear whether Miles had any real interest in aircraft at that stage, and he may have just expected to make some money. Somewhere in the negotiations he was persuaded to accept a swap.

In his book "Miles Aircraft Since 1925", Don L. Brown claimed that when Fred Miles was twenty two he went for a five shilling (25p) joyride at Brighton, and decided that aviation was the life for him. However Miles had his 22nd birthday in 1925, and by that time he was well into the construction of his first biplane. It seems his first flight which so inspired him would have been well before 1925. In his book "Wings Over Woodley", Julian Temple quotes 1922 which makes much better sense.

It is far more likely that following the flight he was then inspired to commence construction of his own plane using some of the components  from the partly-completed Gates-Wallis project. Doubtless many people thought of him as a bit of a madcap, and that he would soon tire of his latest interest. However history was to show otherwise . . .

# *1925*

By the middle of 1925 Miles had almost completed the airframe of his biplane which he called "The Gnat". It appears Fred Wallis got caught up with the project as the longerons for the "Gnat" came from the sports car chassis. Other members of the team included brother Dennis Miles and a friend named Ruben Hart. Ruben Hart had a younger brother named Bert. As a direct result of one conversation Bert had with Charles Gates when he came to Portslade for that historic meeting in 1921, Bert Hart joined the RAF Apprentice scheme. In later years Bert was to join Miles Aircraft, forming yet another link in the chain between the parties in the original team. He worked at Woodley, and then at Redhill before coming to Shoreham in 1952.

As Don L. Brown recorded in his book, the "Gnat" design evolved without drawings, but it was workmanlike and the product of the practical experience of Fred Wallis. They had a small two cylinder engine of 698 c.c. and a four foot diameter propeller which had been used in a plane at the 1923 competitions at Lympne. They had all the ingredients of a plane and great enthusiasm, but as far as it is known they never got round to covering the airframe with fabric, and it never actually flew. It was eclipsed by later events . . .

At that stage Miles still had to learn to fly and Fred Wallis remembered Cecil Pashley who had operated the Flying School at Shoreham before WW I. So Miles went off to London to seek out Cecil Pashley, and while no date is recorded, it seems their first meeting would have been in the late summer of 1925. It says something for Miles and his boundless enthusiasm and persuasive powers that he got Cecil Pashley to agree to a partnership with him to set up a Flying School and joyriding business. The plan was to use Pashley's precious Avro 504K G-EATU, and for F.G. Miles Senior to provide the finance.

The Avro was flown down from Hendon by Pashley on September 25th 1925, and he landed it on a hillside to the north of Portslade (of course no aerodrome was available at Shoreham at the time). It was then dismantled, and taken to the Star Model Laundry where it was completely overhauled. This took them many weeks, and the somewhat unorthodox location probably did not impress the man from the Air Ministry who carried out the survey of their work. Of course Miles was very lucky to have had such an indulgent father who allowed them to use his premises for the work, and it is doubtful whether he would have succeeded without his father's constant support in all their endeavours, and the finance both then and later.

They still had to find a suitable aerodrome in the area, and Miles remembered Wingfield's "Sussex Aero Club" sign which remained on the roof of the barn at New Salts Farm south of the railway line at Shoreham. They managed to persuade Mr. Easter, the farmer, to rent the barn and field to them, despite the fact he was difficult to get on with and did not hold with these new-fangled flying machines which had crashed in and around his farm in the past. (See map of original lease agreement.)

By mid-November 1925 G-EATU was ready, and so it was transported to the barn at "Easter's Field", and the newly formed "Gnat Aero Company" was in residence. The fledgling company started operations immediately G-EATU had been assembled, and the aircraft log book records three short flights on November 24th 1925. A passenger was recorded, but not named, and it is pretty certain it would have been young Miles! Two days later, on November 26th 1925, Pashley began to teach Miles to fly.

As recorded by Don L. Brown, initially things were very primitive as they had to share the field with the farmer's cows which had to be kept at bay with a barbed wire fence! The Air Ministry refused to license the field as an aerodrome presumably because it was so small, and only had a barn for a hangar. At first they had just four pupils and Pashley was very conscious that they had only one aircraft to support the infant business.

By the end of 1925, under the careful tuition of Cecil Pashley, Miles had completed just over 3 hours dual.

## 1926

When the Grahame-White Company at Hendon was sold up Pashley and Miles bought the Bantam G-EAFL and an ancient Grahame-White Boxkite plus a useful range of spares. However hangar accommodation was fast becoming a problem, and so they purchased a Bessoneaux hangar (a canvas hangar used by the RFC in WW I) which they erected next to the barn. Money was tight Pashley was paid just £3 a week, and Miles drew what he needed for current expenses. Pashley, it appears, also helped out on occasions for the purchase of equipment as they went along, probably from his own pocket.

But then realising just how vulnerable they were with just one Avro, they managed to put together a second Avro 504K G-EAJU from spares bought when Avro closed their factory at Hamble. Other Hamble purchases had included an Avro Baby G-EAUM, and also an AvroTriplane.

Late in April 1926 a larger field was found, just north of the railway, which was four hundred yards long and two hundred yards wide, for thirty shillings a week. (See location No.3.) So plans were put in hand to build two hangars and a Clubhouse at the new location. (A local brewery had agreed to donate £100 towards the Clubhouse provided they sold their beer).

However the General Strike of May 5-12th 1926 slowed things down, and while the strike was on, Easter's Field was used by Imperial Airways to fly over copies of the "Daily Mail" which the Newspaper had printed in Paris to by-pass the strikers. Using a D.H.34b (which was possibly G-EBBV, one of two remaining on strength) Captain Dismore of Imperial Airways would land the ten-seater plane powered by a 450 h.p. Napier Lion on the tiny field, and then Miles would drive the consignment into Brighton for distribution.

With the General Strike over and things returning to normal they decided the time was ripe to have a flying display to launch the new aerodrome. They had posters printed for the event which was planned for June 19th 1926.

About this time they acquired two Centaur F4 biplanes G-EABI and G-EALL, for just £30 each. G-EALL was used for joyriding, but it appears G-EABI was kept for spares as there is no mention of it in early log books.

In the meantime Miles had progressed well with his flying instruction from Pashley, and on May 19th 1926 he made his first solo. The flight lasted for 12 minutes in G-EATU. He had spent some 15 hours 24 minutes dual before going solo. (In his book "Miles Aircraft Since 1925", Don Brown claimed that Miles had in fact made his first flight illegally before this date, and pulled the Avro G-EATU out of the barn at Easter's early one morning before anybody was about, and went solo. However, it has not been possible to verify this claim.)

Miles did not fly again until May 22nd when he had a further six short flights in G-EATU. Then on May 24th he had a short four minute dual with Pashley in the Centaur G-EALL followed by three short solo flights, and one on the next day. The Centaur was a docile aircraft to fly, and Miles took up his first passenger for a five minute flight on June 5th 1926 (see Appendix for further details of Miles' early flights)

By June 15th it would appear the move from Easter's Field was nearly complete as Miles did not fly at all between June 15th and June 18th, no doubt busy with the move. The Bessoneaux hangar was dismantled and moved across to the new aerodrome in this period.

However their activities had come to the notice of the authorities, who viewed their somewhat unorthodox operations with suspicion. Only Pashley had a "B" licence for flying for hire or reward, although Miles had taken his "A" licence on a Centaur, and this was issued on June 15th 1926. Nobody it seems had an engineer's licence at that stage, and the less said about Certificates of Airworthiness etc. the better . . .

Don L. Brown described how they received a stern note from the Air Ministry, and one day a bit later a Ministry Bristol Fighter landed, but ran out of aerodrome and ended up in a ditch. Nobody was hurt, but it did not improve their reputation. However nothing more was heard so they pressed on with their plans, and the posters were distributed round the district.

However on the day of the display, and only an hour before the show was due to start, another Bristol Fighter was seen to be circling the aerodrome, and obviously preparing to land. Then it landed, making a perfect touchdown, and out stepped no less a person than Sir Sefton Brancker, the Director of Civil Aviation, complete with monocle!

Miles thought the end had come, but bravely welcomed Sir Sefton and offered him a beer in the new Clubhouse. "So this is the Headquarters of the Independent Air Force?" asked Sir Sefton. "No licences, no Certificates of Airworthiness, no inspections" he boomed!

Humbly Miles told him of their difficulties, and showed him round their workshops in their two home-made wooden hangars. Characteristically Brancker did not close them down as he could have done, but instead he just told them that really things could not go on like that, and got an undertaking from Miles to put his house in order. (It was a tragedy for the struggling aviation entrepreneurs like Miles when Sir Sefton lost his life in the Airship R101 crash four years later).

So the flying display was allowed to go ahead despite all, and the RAF provided aerobatics while Pashley contributed with one perfect loop in his faithful Avro G-EATU. Demonstrations by planes of the day added to the programme, and the day was then completed with joyrides. Miles made six flights with passengers on the day, and a further five next day all in Centaur G-EALL. It may not have been as good as the shows put on by Wingfield in the Flying Meetings of pre-WW I, but at least they had put Shoreham on the map again.

The business was then split in two, with Southern Aircraft Ltd. becoming the parent body looking after maintenance and construction, and the Southern Aero Club Ltd. doing the flying training and joyrides. However they were not to be registered at Companies House until towards the end of 1929, probably due to the cost factor.

Pashley himself was to crash the precious Avro G-EATU at the end of July 1926 when he suffered engine failure on take-off, and ended up in a ditch wrecking the Avro. It was eventually rebuilt, but it was to be some while before it would fly again. His passengers were the Club Secretary, Cecil Boucher, and the ground engineer Hawes, but fortunately nobody was badly hurt. However it was a major disaster for the young company. So Miles rushed off to his father with the bad news. Once more Mr. Miles Senior came to the rescue with £300, and on August 2nd 1926 Miles went off to Brooklands where he collected a replacement Avro G-EBJE previously owned by John Cobb, the racing driver.

G-EBJE was to remain with them for many years, and became Cecil Pashley's exclusive mount for joyrides. It is preserved to this day in the RAF Museum at Hendon in a modified form as a military Avro 504, E 449. Pashley was landing on the beaches and elsewhere in the district offering joyrides. Any open area the size of a cricket pitch served in those days. G-EBJE was used for these outside joyrides while G-EAJU was kept at Shoreham and used for local flights and instructional needs.

To honour their commitment to Sir Sefton Brancker it was agreed that Miles should get his "B" licence as he had completed the necessary 30 hours flying. In his book Don L. Brown describes how Miles used one of the Avros, probably G-EAJU, which had been temporarily fitted with the Bantam engine as the Le Rhone engine of the Avro was being overhauled. However the Bantam engine was only 80 h.p. instead of the normal 110 h.p. of the Le Rhone, and Miles found he was being slowed by headwinds on the final leg of the required 200 miles cross-country flight. So he put down in failing light on a field near Portsmouth, and slept under a hay stack! He returned to Shoreham early next morning, and it appears nobody was very worried as no E.T.A.'s (estimated time of arrival) were given in those days.

Towards the end of the year Berkshire Aviation also took up residence at Shoreham with a pair of Avro 504Ks, G-EAKX and G-EBKX, offering joyrides. The pilots were a pair called Sparks and Beck.

## 1927

During 1927 Miles decided to modify the Avro Baby G-EAUM into a two-seater by installing a larger 60 h.p. Cirrus engine in place of the 35 h.p. Green. This was done without any real knowledge about the centre of gravity. If it looked right it probably was! As it turned out it was a very successful modification.

Miles also purchased an S.E.5A G-EBPA, reaching an altitude of 7000 feet on his delivery flight from Hamble, a Club record at the time.

It was about this time that Sir Alan Cobham was trying to interest Councils about setting up Municipal aerodromes. He wrote to the Worthing Council, but they made no immediate decision.

## 1928

On May 19th 1928 a very ambitious Flying Meeting was held at Shoreham. The Show included some exciting stunt flying by Flight Lieutenant Luxmoore, a former pupil at Lancing College, and also flour bombing of a moving Alvis motor car. A contingent of about fifty members of the Lancing College O.T.C. commanded by Major E.B. Gordon were kitted out as Arab-style natives who defended a dummy fort in the middle of the aerodrome. Flt. Lt. Luxmoore led the aerial attack while boys inside the fort let off very realistic and noisy dummy high-explosive bombs. The end came when the fort dramatically burned down.

The involvement with Lancing College was no doubt due to the fact that Major Gordon ("Gordo" to his Lancing friends) had been taught to fly by Pashley.

The Southern Aero Club continued to flourish. One wealthy member, L.E.R. Bellairs, had an Avro 504K G-EBVL which was promptly nicknamed "Bovril". The owner's "Coat of Arms" was painted on one of the bucket seats; it read "Ferio et feci" or "I strike and have done" which seems hardly appropriate for an aircraft.

At that time, the RAF Squadrons at nearby Tangmere were equipped with Armstrong Whitworth Siskin biplanes, and they were often visitors to Shoreham on cross-country flights.

Younger brother George Miles joined the enterprise during 1928 to help with running repairs and administration. The other Miles identity to join the organisation at this time was Don L. Brown. He was to teach Miles mathematics which was to serve him well in later years. Both learned to fly by degrees, but in between day-to-day activities, and much of it was gained during flights to and from joy-flight operations.

As the Club grew they had acquired the Avro 504Ks previously owned by Berkshire Air Tours, G-EAKX and G-EBKX. (Don Brown had his first flight in G-EBKX in 1926). Lionel Bellairs added to the fleet at Shoreham by purchasing an Avian G-EBVA.

In mid-1928 the Mayor of Worthing met Mr. Miles Senior to discuss the possibility that the old Brighton-Shoreham aerodrome could become the Municipal Airport. Later the same year a Joint Airport Conference was set up with representatives of the three municipalities of Brighton, Hove and Worthing.

## 1929

Miles and Pashley went further afield in the course of joyriding. They operated from a field at Wannock Glen not far from Eastbourne, and also from one near the Railway works at South Lancing. It was there that Miles accidentally turned over Avro G-EBVL, without injury but writing off the aircraft; it was quickly replaced by another, G-EBYB.

Pashley was also giving joyrides from a field adjacent to Roedean School thereby maintaining the link with that school established by Morison and Gilmour back in 1911 . . .

Don Brown recalled in his book how "Pash" would continue joyriding until dusk when business was good, and returned to Shoreham late in the evening, so late on some occasions it became necessary to provide him with flares to enable him to land. Three people would stand in a line across the little field each armed with a two gallon can of petrol. When the sound of the Avro

CECIL LAURENCE PASHLEY ("PASH"), MBE, AFC.
SHOREHAM'S LONGEST SERVING AVIATOR
AND MOST DISTINGUISHED INSTRUCTOR
Photo: Mitchell (taken in the early 1960s).

He held a Pilots licence for nearly sixty years and was an instructor for 55 of those years. He amassed over 20,000 hours as an instructor, probably more than anyone then or since . . . He was awarded the M.B.E., the Royal Aero Club Silver Medal, the Livery of the Guild of Air Pilots and Navigators and was a Freeman of the City of London. He died on December 10th 1969.
(Details from a letter written by Richard Almond to Charles Gates dated May 29th 1979).

The Miles brothers in 1938

F.G. Miles

G.H. Miles

The "Gnat" Biplane in an advanced stage of construction in the
Star Model Laundry, Portslade around 1925. Left to right are:
Dennis Miles, Fred Wallis, Fred Miles, Ru Hart and Cecil
Pashley.
Photo: Miles Aircraft Ltd./Adwest Archives.

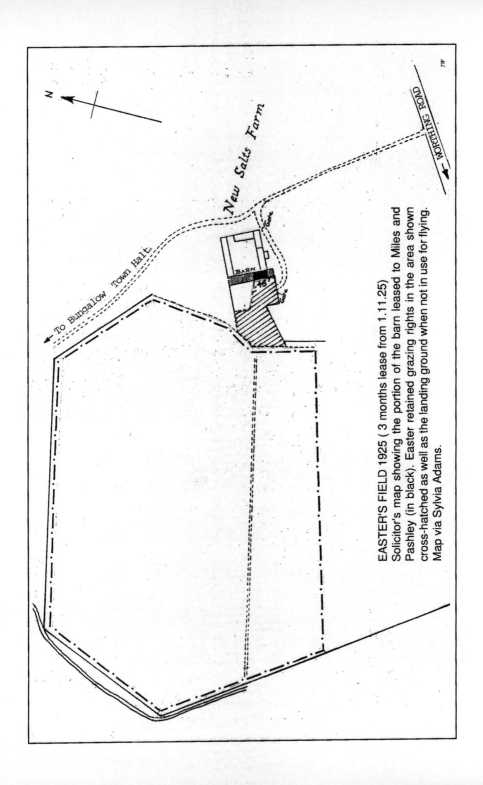

EASTER'S FIELD 1925 ( 3 months lease from 1.11.25)
Solicitor's map showing the portion of the barn leased to Miles and
Pashley (in black). Easter retained grazing rights in the area shown
cross-hatched as well as the landing ground when not in use for flying.
Map via Sylvia Adams.

The early Miles team outside the Bessoneaux hangar at Easter's Field around April 1926. Miles is second from the left, and Cecil Pashley is second from the right. The identities of the others are not known.Pashley's Avro 504 G-EATU is behind the group, and the partly completed G-EAJU can be seen in the hangar. The low building in the centre background is the southern end of the barn which appears in the solicitors map on the previous page. The houses in the background which appear in both these photos were once on the Brighton-Worthing road, but had gone by the time the aerial photo on the next page was taken. This cast some doubt on the actual location of the barn, until Sylvia Adams found the lease agreement and map.
Photo: Miles Aircraft Ltd./Adwest Archives.

This photo is the only other one recording aircraft at Easter's Field. However as the aircraft shown is clearly G-EBJE bought to replace G-EATU in August 1926 several months after they left Easter's Field, it must have been a once only landing to get a photo of operations from Easter's Field.
Photo: Miles Aircraft Ltd./Adwest Archives.

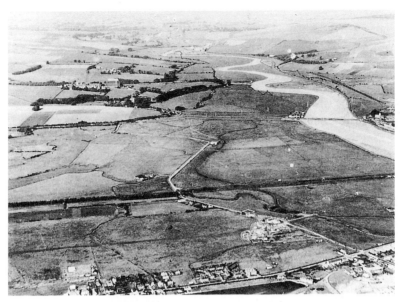

A general view of the area taken around 1930-31. Easter's Field is in the foreground with New Salts Farm on the right. New Salts Farm Road can be seen running to the north with the "new" aerodrome to the left of the road and the 1911-1921 aerodrome site to the right.
Photo: The Shoreham Airport Collection.

An interior view of Easter's barn. Fred Miles is back to the camera on the right, and Cecil Pashley is in the centre of the group at the work bench. Note "Pash" used a wooden block to stand on to make up for his short stature!
Photo: The Shoreham Airport Collection.

Avro 504K G-EAJU built from spares at Easter's Field in 1926.
Photo: "Aeroplane Monthly" Oct. 1979.

Avro 504K G-EBJE which replaced G-EATU after it crashed
it in July 1926. Photo: "Aeroplane Monthly" Oct. 1979.

The Grahame-White Bantam G-EAFL bought by F.G. Miles
in 1926, and in the background the Avro Baby G-EAUM.
Photo: Miles Aircraft Ltd./Adwest Archives.

The Avro 534 Baby which Miles bought in 1927, and later modified into a two-seater with a larger 60 h.p. ADC Cirrus Motor, as seen in this view.

The Avro 504K G-EBVL owned by L.E.R. Bellairs in 1928.

A sudden gust of wind may have been the cause of this incident in the summer of 1928 . . .
All photos: "Aeroplane Monthly" Oct. 1979.

The Austin Whippet G-EAPF bought by Miles
which languished at Shoreham until 1931.

The Sopwith Dove G-EBKY which was a civil variant of
the famous Sopwith Pup. This example seen at Shoreham
in 1929 is now in the Shuttleworth Collection.

The ill-fated Martinsyde F.4 in which Miles
had a narrow escape from disaster in 1929.
All photos: "Aeroplane Monthly" Oct. 1979.

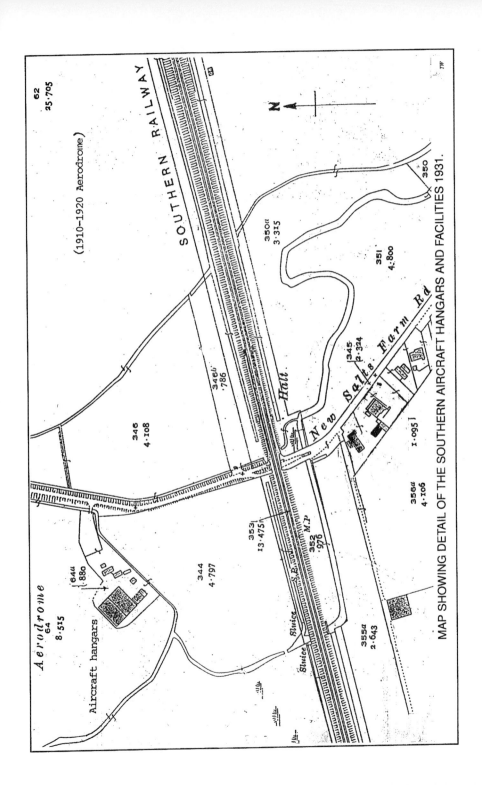

MAP SHOWING DETAIL OF THE SOUTHERN AIRCRAFT HANGARS AND FACILITIES 1931.

engine was heard a little petrol was thrown onto the grass and lit with a match! As Don Brown put it, "It is a testimony to Pashley's skill that, small as the field was with only three little fires to guide him, he never once failed to land successfully at the first attempt."

Shrewdly Miles saw an opportunity to capitalise on the probability that the old Brighton-Shoreham aerodrome would become the proposed Municipal Airport, and he persuaded his father to take out a bank loan for £7000. In June 1929 they bought the 147½ acre site (see location No. 4 in airfield map).

In September 1929 Sir Alan Cobham landed his D.H.61 "Youth of Britain" at "Field Place" on the Littlehampton-Worthing road to promote the National Municipal Aerodrome scheme. Sir Alan flew a number of the local dignitaries around the area, and there is no doubt that he was largely responsible for the eventual establishment of the Municipal Airport at Shoreham.

Also in 1929 Don Brown began his formal flying training on the Avian G-EBVA.

A number of unusual aircraft were at Shoreham during the year including an Austin Whippet G-EAPF. It was designed by the Austin Motor Company in 1919 as a low powered strut-braced biplane with folding wings, but they could find no market for it in the post war era. Other visitors were the Boulton Paul P.2, G-EBEQ, a two-seat high wing Fiat I-AAZB, and also a Sopwith Dove G-EBKY (which survives in the Shuttleworth collection converted to a Pup).

As Don L. Brown recorded in "Miles Aircraft Since 1925", Miles had a lucky escape from disaster in 1929. A Martinsyde F.4 G-EBMI was being assembled, and they had been trying for some time to start the motor. When the motor suddenly fired unexpectedly Miles found himself heading straight towards the petrol pump. Although half in the cockpit, he somehow managed to swing himself into the seat, and turned the Martinsyde away from the pump just in time. Then to his horror he found he could not stop the engine as the ignition switches were disconnected! In moments he was airborne without his belt on, and worse still with only two of the four ailerons connected! He somehow staggered round the circuit, but when he tried to make a landing he found the engine would not throttle back. He resorted to turning off the fuel on the approach, and after one abortive attempt he got it right and landed safely . . .

Also in 1929, Miles embarked on his first completely new design which was based on the Avro Baby. He named it the "Southern Martlet", but wisely got help with the stress calculations from a Horace Miles (no relation) who was attached to the Hendy Aircraft Company which had just set up at Shoreham. The prototype Martlet G-AAII was a single-seat staggered biplane fitted with a 75 h.p. ABC Hornet engine. It was first flown by Miles on July 10th 1929, and was to prove a winner. Eventually six were built to special orders for clients.

In the meantime the Hendy Aircraft Company had also produced a new design at Shoreham. In an article entitled "Gull Genesis" by Ian Harwood published in the "Aeroplane Monthly" of December 1979, the story is told of Basil Henderson, who had patented a novel kind of two-spar wing construction which gave great torsional and bending stiffness, but without excessive weight. They built the new wing in a small shed at Shoreham, and then fitted it to a single-seat monoplane of their own design which they called the Hendy 281 "Hobo." It was fitted with a 35 h.p. Scorpion engine and was registered G-AAIG. It was flown successfully in October that year piloted by Edgar Percival, who was later to form the well-known Percival Aircraft Company. Later they fitted a larger 90 h.p. Pobjoy Cataract radial engine as the Hobo was somewhat underpowered.

Percival had come to England from his native Australia where he had gained considerable experience in the light aircraft field. He had joined forces with the Hendy team to contribute practical advice.

They then decided to design a two-seater development of the Hobo, and a contract was placed with George Parnell at Yate near Bristol to construct the machine which Percival wanted to enter in the 1930 King's Cup Air Race. This machine was known as the Hendy 302, and was registered G-AAVT. It was the forerunner of the famous line of Percival Gulls, and had Percival maintained his link with the Hendy Aircraft Company, the Percival Aircraft Company could well have begun at Shoreham. However he went his own way, and always claimed the Gull design his own despite the obvious lineage from the Hendy 302.

## *1930*

In his book Don Brown described how the Martlet production began in earnest in 1930, and how the second Martlet G-AAVD flew in March 1930. It was powered by a 85 h.p. Armstrong Siddeley Genet radial, and was built for Club member Lionel Bellairs. The third, G-AAYZ, was built for the Right Hon. F.E. Guest, and flown in the 1930 King's Cup, but it had to retire with engine trouble. It had a 120 h.p. Gipsy II. The fourth Martlet G-AAYX was ordered as an aerobatic mount by Flt. Lt. R.L.R. Atcherley, and had a 105 h.p. Armstrong Siddeley Genet five cylinder engine. (However, this order was later cancelled as Miles needed cash up front). The fifth Martlet G-ABBN was ordered by the Duke of Hamilton, and the sixth and last, G-ABIF, was ordered by Mrs. Maxine Freeman-Thomas. (The fourth Martlet G-AAYX survives to this day with the Shuttleworth Trust, and will be airworthy again before long).

On July 24th the wayward Martinsyde was sold to E.D.A. Biggs of the Reading Aero Club, and was collected from Shoreham by their C.F.I. "Pat" Giddy. He was warned to treat it gently because of its age, but sadly this advice was ignored. On arrival at Woodley Giddy did some aerobatics, and the machine broke up in the air; he died of his injuries shortly after.

Another interesting purchase in 1930 was an Avro 548 G-EBKN fitted with a 150 h.p. Airdisco V8 engine driving a large-geared propeller. As a result the aircraft had a very short take-off. Also it was possible to lean over from the front cockpit, and to adjust the twin carburettors in flight! Graham Head, owner of the Avro 548, became honorary Assistant Instructor at Shoreham, and this allowed Miles and Pashley to go further afield for joyriding business. Pashley found a field near Dyke Road Hove, but Miles went much further, and used a field alongside the Lewes to Eastbourne road at Alfriston (near the Drusilla's Tea Gardens).

These were carefree days, and they got away with things which nowadays would be frowned upon. One day a Club member flew over to Drusilla's with his fiancee in the Avian, but had trouble starting it up for the return flight to Shoreham. So Miles offered them a lift in the Avro 504 which normally carried just two passengers. This meant five up including Don Brown and the mechanic on just 110 h.p . . . The take-off was hair-raising towards tall trees, and they only just made it!

Don Brown described in his book how by 1930 Miles had added to his qualifications, having gained his Ground Engineer's licence in categories A, B, C and D in addition to his A and B pilot's licences . . . a rare achievement.

A landing of a Cirrus Moth G-EBZG which ended up in one of Shoreham's famous ditches resulted in the Club buying the wreck for a nominal figure, and they then rebuilt it for their own use. It was later bought by some new Club members, the Hon. Inigo Freeman-Thomas and his wife Maxine (better known as "Blossom").

Miles taught Blossom to fly, and her log book records that her initial flight was in the Avro 504K G-EBYB on June 2nd 1930. She went solo on July 25th after 15 hours 17 mins. Her husband joined the Board of Southern Aircraft Ltd. in the December of that year.

Then an ex-RAF instructor, S.A. (Bill) Thorn was appointed as the Club Instructor (in later years he would become A.V. Roe's Chief Test Pilot, but sadly would be killed in the crash of the Tudor II prototype just after the war). The Club now had three Avro 504Ks, two Desoutters and a Moth.

Towards the end of 1930 the Joint Airport Committee and a Major Mealing of the Air Ministry inspected the proposed site for the new Municipal Airport. Major Mealing indicated a licence would be granted.

## *1931*

In the summer of 1931 Club members began the first attempts at night-flying from Shoreham in the Cirrus Moth which they had christened "Jemimah". They used petrol flares as they did for

Pashley in earlier years, and the ever-adventurous Miles was at the forefront of these first attempts, but as Don Brown recalled, the naturally cautious Pashley did not altogether approve. To keep the flares alight it was necessary to top them up with petrol from time to time, and the trick was to throw on a little at a time. Any attempt to pour it on resulted in a burn back to the pourer!

In the meantime Blossom Freeman-Thomas appears to have rapidly developed as a competent pilot, and a press report of the time announced she would be flying her husband out to India where his father Lord Willenden was to become the next Viceroy.

However, all of these plans were shelved when Miles and Blossom became romantically involved, and the situation became so very embarrassing that Miles felt he could no longer remain at Shoreham. So in August 1931 Miles announced his resignation from Southern Aircraft. He sold up everything, and bought a Spartan biplane which he had shipped out to Cape Town. It was a devastating blow for all at Shoreham as Miles was the leading light and Captain of the ship.

However he had gone, and so George Miles took over the Club assisted by other members, Pashley continued the joyriding, and Bill Thorn did all the flying instruction.

Meanwhile down in Cape Town Miles decided it was the wrong move, and in due course he came back to England. Blossom was eventually divorced by her husband, and later married Miles. They then set up a small office in Sevenoaks, and designed a little single-seat biplane called the "Satyr". So began a life-long partnership which ultimately led to the famous Miles Aircraft Company Ltd.

In 1932 they teamed up with Charles Powis to build the first Miles Hawk at Woodley near Reading, and with them went Harry Hull, the carpenter, who had helped them build the Martlets at Shoreham. The Phillips and Powis Company became their manufacturer for many years.

## 1932

On the weekend of August 6th and 7th 1932, Sir Alan Cobham's National Aviation Display visited Shoreham, and despite the limited size of the aerodrome they used some quite large types which included a twin-engined Handley Page W.10 G-EBMR. There was also the three-engined Airspeed Ferry G-ABSI which had been specially designed for Sir Alan by A.F. Tiltman. Cobham's fleet also included a Cierva C.19 autogyro which jumped into the air after a remarkably short run. Another feature of the show was Martin Hearn, a wing-walker, who rode on the top wing of an Avro 504K, G-AAAF. (This act was later banned by the Air Ministry).

It is probably not realised just how many towns were visited by Sir Alan's National Air Display during 1932. By the time his "Circus" had reached Shoreham for the Brighton stop he had already visited 106 towns in that year alone, and would finish the year with a staggering 175! In the following year he ran two tours simultaneously, a truly magnificent contribution to make the people of Britain air-minded.

The first scheduled service between Shoreham and the Isle of Wight was commenced in October 1932 by Portsmouth, Southsea and Isle of Wight Aviation Ltd. with a schedule of four flights a day. However little is known of their activities or the aircraft used. As it was well before the new Municipal Airport was established, only small aircraft would have been involved.

## 1933

The future of the Municipal Airport was assured when the joint Airport Committee finally decided to purchase the 147½ acre site bought by Miles Senior in 1929. They paid £10,000 for the land, and set aside a further £31,000 for a new Terminal Building and hangars.

Sir Alan Cobham's Circus was back again twice during the year with two tours. Tour No. 2 visited on June 17-18th, and Tour No.1 made a one day visit on August 13th.

The first visit by a member of the Royal family occured on July 4th 1933 when H.R.H. the Prince of Wales landed at Shoreham.

The first Southern Martlet under construction in the Southern Aircraft hangar at Shoreham in 1928. Left to right: George Miles, Lionel Bellairs,in centre with drawings Don L. Brown and F.G. Miles, beyond the fuselage is Cecil Pashley, and on the extreme right is Harry Hull.
Photo: Miles Aircraft Ltd./Adwest Archives.

The completed Southern Martlet prototype G-AAII taken outside the rear of the hangar it was built in, looking south-east.
Photo: The Shoreham Airport Collection.

Two views of the Hendy 281 Hobo at Shoreham in 1929.

The Hendy 302 prototype. The family resemblance to the later Percival Gull series is evident.

The Avro 548 fitted with a 150 h.p. Airdisco V-8 engine.
All photos by courtesy of the Riding Photograph Collection.

Photo: The Shoreham Airport Collection.

# SOUTHERN AIRCRAFT AERODROME, SHOREHAM, EARLY 1930's

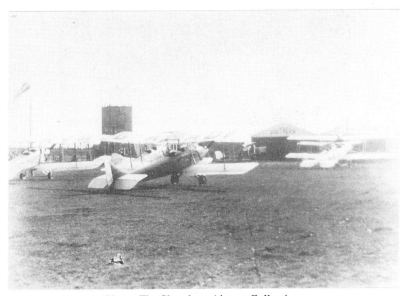

Photo: The Shoreham Airport Collection.

Blossom and F.G. Miles at the drawing board in their office
at Sevenoaks during 1933.
Photo: Miles Aircraft Ltd./Adwest Archives.

This view of the Miles M.1 Satyr emphasizes its small size.
It was powered by a 70 h.p. Pobjoy R and had an all up
weight of only 900 lb.
Photo: Miles Aircraft Ltd./Adwest Archives.

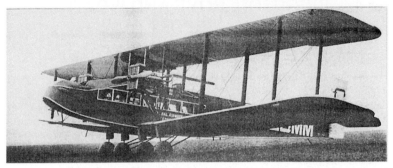

A 16-seater Handley Page W.10, similar to the one used by Sir Alan Cobham's National
Aviation at Shoreham in 1932.
Photo: "The Illustrated Encyclopedia of Aircraft".

The prototype Airspeed Ferry which was specially designed for Sir Alan Cobham
by A.F. Tiltman.
Photo: The Shoreham Airport Collection.

This photo was taken by Don Brown and shows the wing-walker
Martin Hearn in the course of his act during the1932 National
Air Display at Shoreham.

# Chapter 4   BRIGHTON, HOVE AND WORTHING MUNICIPAL AIRPORT (1934-39)

## 1934

Plans were drawn up for the new Terminal Building by Stavers H. Tiltman who also designed Airport buildings at Leeds-Bradford and Belfast Harbour. A two-story Terminal Building was proposed employing the contemporary art-deco style and four hangars. However only one main hangar was eventually built (see map in following pages). Tenders were accepted from James Bodle Ltd. and the final costs were £29,000 for the Terminal Building plus a further £11,889 for improvements to the landing ground, and another £8,278 for other services. Work commenced in the November of 1934.

In the meantime Sir Alan Cobham's Circus had been back at Shoreham on August 18-19th for another week-end's display. In these later Tours a H.P. Clive III, G-ABYX, was used for passenger flights in place of the H.P. W.10 G-EBMR.

## 1935

By March 1935 the steel frame for the Terminal Building had been erected, and good progress had been made upgrading the landing ground and improving the drainage. However, the northern end of the new aerodrome was to remain a drainage problem for some time, and photos of the time show boundary gable markers limiting the landing area. The problem remained until 1941 when extensive drainage works were carried out.

On March 31st Miles flew into Shoreham with one of his latest products, the Miles M.4 Merlin, still carrying its U 8 markings used at the time for new prototypes; it subsequently became G-ADFE. It was very similar to the Falcon series, but it had a wider rear fuselage with seating for three people.

Olley Air Services of Croydon were appointed to run the new Airport, and Railway Air Services included Shoreham in their new timetables in anticipation of commencing operations at an early date. The Southern Railway backed up the preparations by re-opening the Bungalow Town Halt, re-naming it "Shoreham Airport".

Excellent progress was made with construction, and soon the new hangars were also taking shape. By May Railway Air Services had begun operations from Shoreham with two internal flights a day. The Terminal Building was completed ahead of schedule, and the new Airport was ready for use on September 1st 1935.

One week later on September 8th, the 1935 King's Cup Air Race was staged at Hatfield and the still new range of Miles aircraft achieved considerable success. Tommy Rose came in first in the prototype Miles Falcon 6 G-ADLC, and both second and third places went to Miles Hawk Trainers. In all no less than 13 Miles aircraft had been entered, including the Miles Sparrowhawk G-ADNL flown by Fred Miles, which won the elimination race. Flushed with success competitors like Tommy Rose and Fred Miles flew down to the newly-opened Shoreham Airport soon after the race. One of the competitors, a Mrs Battye flying a Hawk Major, overshot on landing and had to be dragged out of one of Shoreham's ditches.

The Southern Aero Club was reconstituted as The South Coast Flying Club under the control of Brooklands Aviation. Club rooms were established on the first floor of the brand new Terminal Building, and a Grand Inaugural Dinner was held to mark the occasion.

Southern Aircraft was then wound up, but the old wooden hangars remained on site for nearly another year. However, another prominent landmark known as Lee's Barn, which was situated on the corner of New Salts Farm Road on the western side of the new Airport, was soon removed, being a considerable hazard to aircraft.

Cecil Pashley became the CFI with the South Coast Flying Club, but George Miles went to join his brother at Woodley who was busy designing and developing the Miles Hawk Trainers and Falcons at Phillips and Powis.

Don Brown also left the scene, but many years later in 1942, he would also end up at Woodley, when he became Personal Assistant to George Miles and was involved with much of their test flying.

## 1936

The official opening of the new Brighton, Hove and Worthing Municipal Airport (as it was styled) was delayed until mid-1936 to allow time to organise an international rally supported by aerobatics from the RAF.

It was during this period the author recalls accompanying his parents on an official tour of the new Airport. A rather suave official showed them round, and this included a visit to the Control Tower, and sitting in an Olley Air Services Short Scion G-ADDO in the brand new hangar. His father was then offered a free flight in a D.H.60 Moth of the South Coast Flying Club, and somewhat reluctantly he went aloft while Mother and two sons watched in awe.

It was only a few weeks later when a similar D.H.60 spun in on Lancing Hill (Boiler Hill to Lancing boys) behind Lancing College. All the locals including the author went up to see the wreck. At the time he and his friends were aeroplane-mad, and he had a beautiful model D.H.89A Rapide loyally painted in the colours of the South Coast Flying Club; so it was taken to the crash site, and shown to the Official who had so recently shown them round the Airport. To the author's dismay the man was not the least bit impressed . . .

In the meantime the brand new Airport with its sparkling white Terminal Building attracted additional air services with both Channel Island Airways and Jersey Airlines establishing regular schedules. Destinations serviced from Shoreham in this period included Bournemouth, Bristol, Cardiff, Croydon, Deauville, Jersey, Le Touquet, Liverpool, Manchester, Portsmouth and Ryde.

Full customs facilities were available. There was an illuminated landing "T" positioned on the western boundary, and a large beacon on the apex of the western end of the hangars flashed "S" for Shoreham at night. Even nearby Lancing College Chapel was equipped with two red lights.

The air was full of D.H.60 Moths and Tiger Moths of the South Coast Flying Club. They had a striking colour scheme of red and black fuselages (the upper decking being red), and silver wings with red letters. Privately owned aircraft included many different types such as Puss Moths, Leopard Moths, and Hornet Moths from the D.H. stable as well as a few Vega Gulls and Miles Falcons etc. The twin-engined planes of the times were Monospars, D.H.84 Dragons, D.H.89A Rapides and the Short Scion of Olley Air Services.

The new Airport was officially opened on June 13th 1936 by the Mayors of Brighton, Hove and Worthing. The day began with a dawn patrol, and was marked by a large gathering of aircraft taking part in the International Rally. A full air display was staged, and aircraft from 19 Squadron of the RAF presented an aerobatic routine.

Cecil Pashley once more had a prominent role opening the display with some crazy flying (see report from the "Worthing Herald" of June 20th 1936 in the Appendix).

The 1936 King's Cup used Shoreham as a control point. One contestant, Peter Reis, had a nose-over on landing and bent his propeller.

One day in the summer of 1936 the vast bulk of the German LZ 129 Zeppelin "Hindenburg" passed over Shoreham at around 1500 feet on a westerly course and presumably headed for New York. What it was doing passing just to the north of the airfield boundary at circuit height is not known, but it never passed that way again as in May 1937 it was to meet with a disastrous end, catching fire on arrival in New York with tragic loss of life.

## 1937

In 1937 The Air Ministry strongly favoured the use of civilian organisations in the major expansion of aircrew training. So it was that the Martin School of Air Navigation, which had set up at Shoreham, received a contract to train RAF Volunteer Reserve pilots commencing July 1st 1937. It was designated No. 16 E & RFTS (Elementary and Reserve Flying Training School) under No. 26 (T) Group.

Two new Bellman-type hangars were erected to the east of the Terminal Building parallel to the railway line. These housed the fleet of RAF Tiger Moths, and later Hawker Harts and Hinds. Standard Air Ministry wooden huts were erected in front of the hangars, and these served as classrooms.

One of the largest visitors to use Shoreham at that time came late in the year in the form of a majestic Imperial Airways four-engined Handley Page H.P.42 G-AAXD which landed on a proving flight from Croydon.

The airline services built up steadily during 1937, and John A. Bagley who wrote "Shoreham and Ford: A History of Two Sussex Airfields", quotes 1,429 flights carrying 6,308 passengers.

## 1938

On January 24th 1938, an RAF Gloster Gladiator from Kenley, flown by Pilot-Sergeant Ernest Lomax, was performing loops high over Hove when he got into a uncontrollable spin. He had to bale out, and came down by parachute, landing on Beaconsfield Road in Hove. He narrowly missed the electric railway line, but his fall was cushioned by hitting tram wires. In the meantime his machine pancaked into the garden of No. 4 Lyndhurst Corner, but only caused slight damage. The "Evening Argus" reported the incident in a full-page spread complete with photos.

Also in 1938 the HT electricity supply lines along the northern boundary near the Sussex Pad were put underground to remove the hazard to north-south aircraft movements.

The increased movements in and out of Shoreham at this time made radio communication vital, and a radio room was added at the rear of the Control Tower. To cope with increased demand, Channel Island Airways introduced the larger four engined D.H.86bs on their run to the Channel Islands.

In May 1938 Navigation Training for bomber pilots was commenced, and Fairey Battles appeared to augment the fleet. Martins hired three D.H.89a Rapides and one D.H.84 Dragon from Airwork for the training. They were specially modified for navigational work with a drift sight let into the floor, and a large chart table. Training flights were made mostly over the sea, and the crew consisted of a civilian pilot and radio operator, and two RAF pupils. One of the pilots employed at the time was R.H. McIntosh, later a Wing Commander, who wrote "All Weather Mac" in which he describes the intense activity at Shoreham in 1938. On one occasion in a "training" exercise over the sea they spotted part of the German fleet which had ventured into the Channel for the first time since the 1914-18 war.

From time to time the large bombers of the day such as Handley Page Heyfords made landings taking part in exercises.

In June 1938 an Imperial Airways Handley Page H.P.42 G-AAXC made a forced landing because of fog at Croydon, and remained overnight while the passengers completed their journey from Paris by road.

Among the more interesting smaller visitors to land at Shoreham in 1938 was the B.A. Eagle G-AFAX which was later flown out to the far east, and eventually found its way to Australia in 1939. Its amazing subsequent history is related in the photo pages at the end of this chapter.

Railway Air Services combined with Channel Air Ferries in December 1938 to form Great Western & Southern Airlines with headquarters at Shoreham.

Also in December full-time training for Observers was commenced by Martins as more and more emphasis was placed on military training, with war clouds looming once again in the history of Shoreham.

## 1939

It appears that Martins were not very efficient as they soon lost the contract for Observer training, and the work went to Airwork at Staverton. However they retained the VR training contract right up to September 1st 1939.

By 1939 "Pash" had accumulated some 10,000 hours and a special dinner was arranged in his honour at the Grand Hotel in Brighton. He was presented with a cheque for 170 guineas (about £85 in today's money), and his old pupil "FG" made the presentation. In his remarks about "Pash," Miles admitted that he did not consider himself as one of Pashley's star pupils by being the first person in the world to be summoned for dangerous flying. He was convicted of low flying over Worthing. (The presentation was fully reported in the "Brighton and Hove Herald", but the press-cutting found in Richard Almond's scrapbooks did not record the actual date.)

On May 20th 1939, an Empire Air Day was put on at Shoreham. Modern warplanes of the day included Vildebeest, Swordfish and Walrus planes from the Navy and Hurricanes and Defiants from the RAF.

War clouds gathered steadily, and on September 3rd 1939 war with Germany was declared. Overnight all VR Training at Shoreham ceased as it was considered too vulnerable to enemy attack. No. 16 E & RFTS was sent to reinforce other E & RFTS s in safer areas.

All Flying Club activity and private flying ceased as well, and so once more Cecil Pashley had to leave Shoreham because of war. This time he went off to South Africa where he trained hundreds of pilots under the Empire Air Training Scheme. All the Flying Club aircraft and the privately owned ones at Shoreham were taken over by the Government, and pressed into service with the RAF.

Shoreham then became elevated to the status of an International Airport under the control of The National Air Communications Organisation handling all the normal Croydon traffic. London was considered to be a high risk area, and airliners from the then neutral countries were painted in high visibility orange paint. Planes of KLM, Sabena and DDL of Denmark were required to go under camouflage nets on arrival much to the annoyance of their Captains who felt it was not their war.

Channel Island Airways and Jersey Airlines took fright and cancelled all their flights to the Channel Islands.

The National Air Communications Organisation operated D.H.91 Albatross aircraft on a Shoreham-Tunis-Alexandria run which was later extended to India. From time to time Armstrong Whitworth Ensigns lumbered in and out of Shoreham although the airfield dimensions were marginal for the type, which was underpowered. Other types seen in this period included D.C.2s, D.C.3s, Lockheed 10A and 14s and Fokker F.X.11s.

In October the flights to and from the Channel Islands were resumed when it appeared the Germans did not intend an immediate attack. Imperial Airways routed their H.P.42s through Shoreham on a run from Heston via Shoreham to Dieppe and on to Paris. Just before Christmas 1939 there were several H.P.42s at Shoreham, and one of them was seen by the author suffering the indignity of having RAF roundels painted on its fuselage prior to becoming a troop carrier.

They were heady days full of tension, and no one quite knew what to expect. Air raid sirens wailed, but they were false alarms. Many felt Shoreham would be attacked at any time despite the heavy green paint daubed over the beautiful new Terminal Building and hangars. Shoreham would be all too easy to find, despite the camouflage, being located alongside the railway line and the River Adur.

As it turned out Shoreham escaped raids in this period, and it would be the October of 1940 before the first attack came. Shoreham would continue in its role as an International Airport for another six months until the German invasion of France finally ended all that, and the airfield came under the control of the RAF for the duration.

**END OF PART 2**

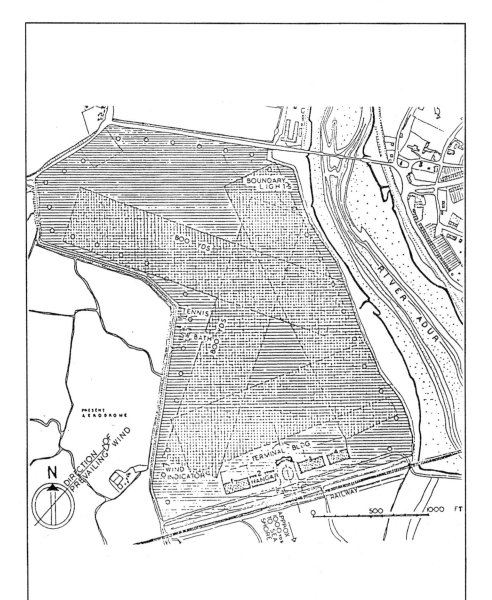

THE ORIGINAL SITE PLAN FOR THE NEW MUNICIPAL AIRPORT
(From Tiltman Staver's report to Worthing Council)

Four hangars were originally proposed, and there was provision for grass runways as shown. However, the NW/SE runway was in an area subject to flooding and often became boggy in wet weather. It was never developed. While No 2 hangar was the only one built to the west of the Terminal Building, hangars No. 3 and No. 4 were eventually built in 1937 when No. 16 EFTS was established.

KING'S CUP AIR RACE, SEPTEMBER 7–8TH 1935
Success for Miles aeroplanes. This photo is believed to have been taken after the race was
over, when the winning aircraft visited Shoreham. The winning Falcon G-ADLC, flown by
Tommy Rose, is on the right. The other aircraft could be the Sparrowhawk G-ADNL flown
by F.G. Miles who won the eliminating race. Altogether 13 Miles types entered the race. In
the foreground is the Olley Air Services Short Scion G-ADDO and a Gipsy Moth G-AADA
of the South Coast Flying Club.
Photo: The Shoreham Airport Collection.

Visiting aircraft parked to the east of the Terminal Building after the 1935 King's Cup. At
the time the new Airport had only been open for use one week!
Photo: The Shoreham Airport Collection.

PANORAMIC COMPOSITE VIEWS FROM THE TERMINAL BUILDING TAKEN ON THE OPENING DAY, JUNE 13th 1936.

The remains of Lee's barn show as a white patch in the background and the gable-end boundary markers show the limit of the landing ground at the time.

Photos: The Shoreham Airport Collection.

The Flying Flea or "Pou du Ciel" seen at Shoreham after taking part in a race on the opening day. The owner, F/O A.C. Clauston, took his dachshund with him! (see item in Appendix under press reports).
Photo: The Shoreham Airport Collection.

Mrs Batty's Hawk Major being towed out of the ditch following an overshoot after the 1935 King's Cup race.
Photo: The Shoreham Airport Collection.

The halcyon days at Shoreham Airport in the summer of 1936 with visitors
enjoying refreshments on the apron. The D.H. 89A Rapide G-ACPR of Railway
Air Services is about to leave with passengers.
Photo: The Shoreham Airport Collection.

Another view of the Terminal Building with two Vega Gulls parked in the foreground. Note
the RAF Tiger Moth being refuelled at the new dispensing point in the background.
Photo: The Shoreham Airport Collection.

Right:
The Caudron 3 biplane OO-ELA seen here at Shoreham after being flown over from Brussels by Ken Waller for the opening of the Municipal Airport. It was built in France in 1912, and had a 100 h.p. Anzani engine.
Photo: John White.

Left:
Cierva C. 19 Autogyro G-ACIO seen here at Shoreham. Note the nose of an Airspeed Envoy on the right.
Photo: John White.

Right:
Railway Air Services D.H. 89A G-ACYM in evening light at Shoreham in 1936.
Photo: John White.

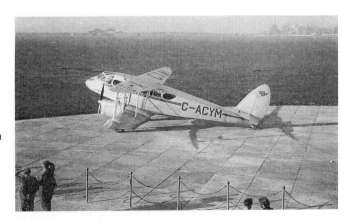

Right:
Railway Air Services D.H 84 Dragon G-ADDI "City of Cardiff" on arrival at Shoreham in 1936. This particular plane survived the war and was later exported to the U.S.A.; it still exists there as N34DH.
Photo: John White.

Left:
Olley Air Service's Short Scion Mk. II G-ADDO powered by two Pobjoy Niagara engines. In 1936 the author sat in this aircraft during a tour of the Airport.
Photo: John White.

Right:
The Monospar G-AEGX named "Florence Nightingale" seen here at Shoreham in 1936. (Note the Lancing College boy in the blazer of the time.)
Photo: John White.

Right:
This B.A.Eagle G-AFAX seen here at Shoreham in 1938 is of interest. It was unique in having a fixed undercarriage instead of the retractable units of the later-model Eagles. It was flown out to Burma in 1939 by Jack Hodder, and when the Japanese invaded he flew it to

Darwin. It remained in Australia as VH-ACN for many years, before returning to the UK about 1977. It visited Shoreham again in 1995 after restoration to G-AFAX.
Photo: John White.

Left:
The Wicko GM.1 G-AEZZ with a Gipsy Major engine in place of the Ford engine. One of a batch made in England to the design of Foster Wickner in Australia.
Photo: John White.

Right:
Aeronca C.3 G-ADSP was one of 16 imported from the U.S.A. It was a popular ultra-light with an engine of only 36 h.p.
Photo: John White.

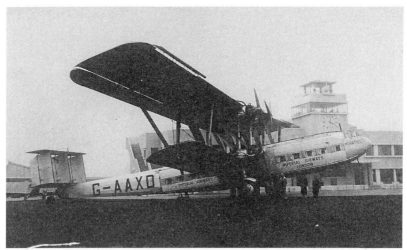

Imperial Airways Handley Page HP. 42 G-AAXD seen at Shoreham late in 1937 when it
landed on a proving flight.
Photo: The Shoreham Airport Collection.

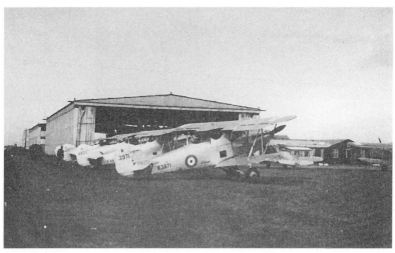

The two Bellman hangars erected in 1937 east of the Terminal Building for the Martin
School of Air Navigation contract. No. 16 E & RFTS Hawker Harts in the foreground; later
Fairey Battles joined the fleet. These hangars only lasted until 1941 when they were bombed
by the Luftwaffe.
Photo: The Shoreham Airport Collection.

# EMPIRE AIR DAY, SHOREHAM MAY 20th 1939

Some of the military types in the aircraft park. Left to right: Fairey Swordfish, Vickers
Vildebeest and Hawker Hurricane.
Photo: The Shoreham Airport Collection.

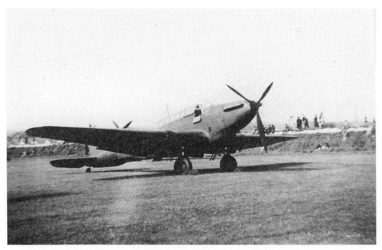

A Fairey Battle light bomber. These were very underpowered and did not
survive very long in operations when war came.
Photo: The Shoreham Airport Collection.

# WONDERS OF WORLD AVIATION

## 7ᴰ WEEKLY

TO BE COMPLETED IN ABOUT 45 WEEKLY PARTS

The D.H. 86 G-ACZN of Jersey Airways makes a fine study as it takes off from Shoreham bound for the Channel Islands in 1938.
Photo: Front cover from "Wonders of World Aviation" April 5th 1938, via Peter Amos.

# Part 3 (1940–1952)

## Chapter 5    WORLD WAR II (1940–1945)

### 1940

During the "phoney war" in the early part of 1940 Shoreham continued in its role as an International Airport. However the tendency to flooding in wet weather was always a problem, and many of the heavier aircraft became bogged at the northern end which had been opened up to provide a longer take-off run. During February and March in 1940 all the services had to be transferred to Tangmere.

On February 10th 1940, the first German bomber appeared over Shoreham when a lone Dornier 17 crossed the airfield at 300 ft., and was engaged by ground defences. No bombs were dropped, and the raider made off. There were similar incidents on February 13th and March 8th, but no damage was recorded. Probably they were all just reconnaissance flights.

German aircraft were hardly welcome at Shoreham at this time, but by a strange twist of fate there was a German-built FW 200A Condor OY-DAM operated by the Danish Airline DDL, and it was operating the run between Copenhagen-Amsterdam-Shoreham during April 1940. However when Germany invaded Denmark on April 9th 1940 it was impounded by the newly formed BOAC and became G-AGAY for a short while before being pressed into service with the RAF.

Members of Lancing College OTC were sent down to the airfield to help dig trenches and defence ditches. While they were thus employed a small plane staggered into Shoreham, and out stepped three Poles who had somehow escaped from Poland, and run the gauntlet of the Germans. One had a bullet wound in his arm. Gordon Flex, who was a boy at Lancing at the time, recalls how the Poles ran over to them for help (confusing the OTC uniforms for the British Army), and while the Poles could not speak English, sign language soon got things sorted out. Next day the Head Master, Frank Doherty, told the whole school of the incident.

Continental services ground to a halt in May 1940 when Germany invaded Belgium and Holland. Finally when Italy entered the war on June 10th 1940, the Middle East route was suspended, and thus Shoreham's short life as an International Airport came to an end.

Following the Dunkirk evacuation in early June 1940, there were very real fears of invasion by the Germans. After the war German plans for the invasion were found, and it showed that the airfield at Shoreham and Shoreham harbour were to be the objectives for a landing in the area.

On June 20th Lancing College up on the hill overlooking the airfield said goodbye to its boys who went to Shropshire for the duration. For a short while in 1940 General Montgomery used the College as his Headquarters. Then the Royal Navy took over, and established H.M.S. King Alfred as a RNVR training depot for the remainder of the war.

Shoreham was then requisitioned by the Air Ministry as an advanced airfield in the Kenley sector of No. 11 Group, Fighter Command. Initially Shoreham was used by Lysanders of No. 225 Squadron on anti-invasion duties flying on coastal patrols.

During August 1940 the air war gradually built up, and there were frequent raids by Me 109s and dog-fights would develop. A report in the "Brighton and Hove Gazette" of August 17th 1940 describes how one Me 109 was brought down in a dog-fight with a Hurricane over Shoreham. The German pilot, Oberleutnant Paul Temme, glided down with his tank on fire preparing to crash-land, but as he came in he had one more go at his foes, and shot-up troops on Bungalow Town beach, but did not hit anyone. He then crash-landed into a cornfield just south of the railway behind the main hangars at Shoreham. He may even have been trying to crash-land on the airfield. Ironically he then had to surrender to the same troops he had just been firing on!

No. 11 Group Fighter Command was to bear the brunt of the Battle of Britain. However,

Shoreham was not a base for Fighter Squadrons at that stage so it did not figure in that battle to any great degree, but its former sister Airport at Croydon was attacked on August 15th 1940 with a heavy loss of life; at that time it was a satellite airfield of RAF Kenley.

One of Shoreham's former identities from WW I, Stanley Vincent, by then a Group Captain commanding the Northolt sector, had the satisfaction of seeing German bombers over London turn back as the result of his single-handed head-on attack at the height of the Battle.

On August 20th 1940, the Fighter Interception Unit (FIU) was bombed out of Tangmere, and moved to Shoreham with their sole surviving Beaufighter. A few days later this was joined by a second all-black Beaufighter R 2059. They flew night sorties for a short period from September 1st, but the unit had some problems. When Flying Officer G. Ashfield made his first sortie on the night of September 4/5th 1940 his AI (Airborne Interception) unit failed. This was an early form of radar. On the night of September 12/13th, R 2059 failed to return from a sortie over the French coast.

On the evening of October 8th 1940 Shoreham had its first serious attack by the Luftwaffe when three Me.109s dropped bombs and machine-gunned the ground defences. It is not known whether there were any casualties, but there was some damage and the airfield was temporarily out of action.

The Beaufighters were withdrawn on October 14th, and replaced by Hurricanes of No. 422 Flight. As a night fighter unit they enjoyed much greater success. Accommodation for units based at Shoreham was non-existent at the time, so the nearby Sussex Pad Hotel became the Officers' Mess, and Ricardo's Engineering Works near the Adur River bridge became the Sergeants' Mess. Most of the airmen were billeted with families in the area.

There was another minor bombing attack at 4.30 a.m. on December 4th, when a single HE bomb was dropped, but without damage.

## *1941*

In January 1941 No. 422 Flight moved from Shoreham to Cranage near Manchester having destroyed two enemy aircraft and damaged another in their short stay. The FIU also left a short time later and went to Ford.

It was then decided to increase the size of the airfield which only offered an 800 yard maximum run north to south. Extensions were made to the west by levelling New Salts Farm Road embankment which formed the western boundary at that time. The notorious ditches went underground in concrete pipes, and the old 1926-1935 aerodrome was also incorporated plus a strip of land beyond to the S.W. corner. This gave a much improved landing run of some 1200 yards on 04/22 (or N.E. to S.W.).

However, all this activity caught the eye of the Luftwaffe, and on March 13th 1941 Shoreham was attacked again by seven Me.109s at 7.15 a.m., dropping HE bombs and machine-gunning in earnest. A short time later two more 109s strafed the airfield with cannon from 200 ft., doing slight damage to the hangars and buildings.

On March 26th a lone raider attacked at about 6 p.m. dropping six HE bombs across the airfield, two of which did not explode. This aircraft also machine-gunned, but did no damage. It is thought that the unexploded bomb which was discovered 42 years later in 1982 was one of these. It was found under the centre-line of the former grass runway 08/26, in the middle of the airfield (see historical map of the airfield). That bomb (minus its lethal charge) now resides in the Terminal Building on display.

The only resident aircraft at Shoreham in this period were Lysanders of 1488 Fighter Gunnery (FG) Flight, and a detachment from 225 Squadron. There were numerous air-raid warnings, and while most did not develop, German aircraft were often in the area. On April 8th a lone Me 109 dropped two HE bombs, but they fell outside the airfield boundary not far away.

However on the night of May 8/9th 1941 there was a much more determined attack. Just after midnight ten HE 250 kg bombs were dropped on Shoreham, destroying the main hangars and putting the airfield out of action. Somehow they missed the Terminal Building, but it is probable they also badly damaged the two Bellman hangars erected in 1937 for No. 16 E & EFTS. No details of casualties are known, but it was a severe attack, and possibly carried out by He 111s.

It was then decided to build four new "Over Blister" hangars, and to disperse them round the airfield perimeter rather than rebuilding the main hangars. One was built under the skeleton remains of the main hangars, another was erected in the S.E. corner, and two opposite the Sussex Pad. Also a new perimeter road was laid along the eastern and northern boundaries to connect the new hangars. (In 1991 this road was named "Cecil Pashley Way" as a tribute to Shoreham's most distinguished aviator). Two large hard standings were also built on the eastern boundary adjacent to the river bank.

A new Battle H.Q. was built on the bank overlooking the airfield just to the west of the Sussex Pad. In later years it was the ideal place for plane-spotting for boys at Lancing College, but it was removed when the A 27 bypass was built.

An Air Sea Rescue (ASR) Flight of two Lysanders was then established. They carried a dinghy pack on each bomb rack, and smoke floats under the fuselage. They quickly proved themselves valuable in locating baled-out crews up to 20 miles off-shore.

Six more Lysanders arrived in October 1941, but these were used by No 1488 Flight for target-towing duties. Their task was to provide air-to-air firing practice for local Fighter Squadrons.

In December 1941 both units were rationalised into 277 ASR Squadron with the addition of two Walrus amphibians and another Lysander. 277 Squadron had been formed at Stapleford Tawney in Essex that month from detachments at Shoreham, Hawkinge, Tangmere, Martlesham Heath, Kenley and Stapleford Tawney.

Stapleford Tawney served as the H.Q. base, with A Flight at Martlesham Heath, B Flight at Hawkinge and C Flight at Shoreham. In 1942 the H.Q. base would move to Gravesend, and then to Shoreham in 1944. 277 ASR Squadron covered the North Sea areas off Essex and the English Channel round to the Isle of Wight; thus it was right in the forefront of the war. The Squadron motto was "Quaerendo Servamus" (we save by seeking), and had the code BA.

Details of the more interesting rescues carried out by C Flight of 277 Squadron which appear in the following pages are a blend of reports from various sources. In particular many come from "Another Kind of Courage", the excellent story of the ASR, written by Norman Franks and published by Patrick Stephens Ltd. Permission to use the material is gratefully acknowledged.

## 1942

On February 9th 1942 Flight 1488 moved to Southend, but a detachment remained at Shoreham. They were constantly plagued with the spares problem, and in particular the lack of Lysander replacement tailplanes.

One of the first "customers" for the 277 Flight at Shoreham was Grp. Cpt. Richard Atcherley who had to ditch his Spitfire in the English Channel with engine trouble. Sgt. Tom Fletcher flew out in a Lysander, and directed a trawler to pick him up (This was the same Richard Atcherley who had ordered one of the Miles Martlets back in 1930.)

On May 1st 1942 Flt. Sgt. Holland, flying one of the new ASR Walrus amphibians, successfully located Flt. Lt. Neal of Biggin Hill and brought him safely back to Shoreham. The ability of the Walrus to both locate and rescue pilots was quickly appreciated.

In May it was decided to replace some of the Lysanders with Defiants. This decision may have been prompted by the lack of spares for the Lysanders, and their poor serviceability record. However, the Defiants were none too popular with the crews as they lacked the slow speed of the high-wing Lysander which made them so suitable for spotting downed pilots. In combat the Defiant had no forward firing guns, and were no match for Me.109s and FW 190s.

On May 26th the pilot of a Spitfire from No. 12 Squadron made a spectacular "belly landing" with damaged elevator controls and part of the port elevator shot away. Another Spitfire pilot

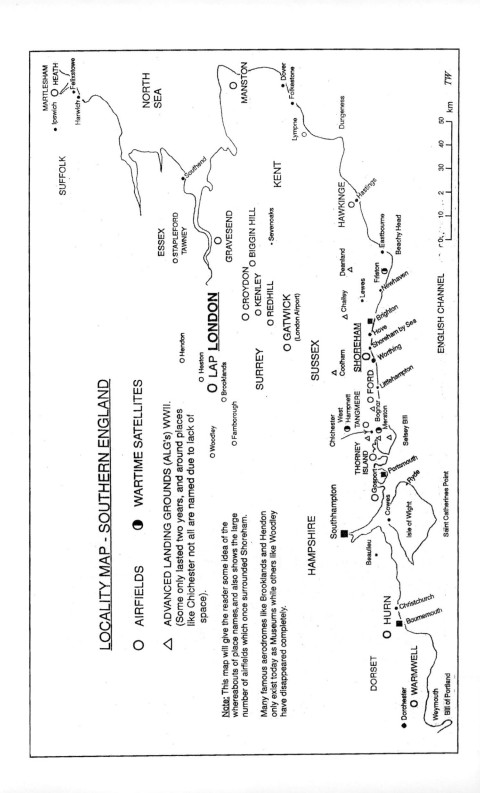

LOCALITY MAP - SOUTHERN ENGLAND

○ AIRFIELDS        ● WARTIME SATELLITES

△ ADVANCED LANDING GROUNDS (ALG's) WWII.
(Some only lasted two years, and around places
like Chichester not all are named due to lack of
space).

Note: This map will give the reader some idea of the
whereabouts of place names, and also shows the large
number of airfields which once surrounded Shoreham.

Many famous aerodromes like Brooklands and Hendon
only exist today as Museums while others like Woodley
have disappeared completely.

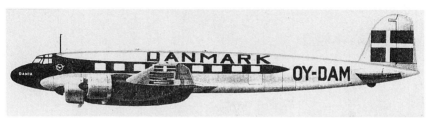

This Focke-Wulf FW. 200A Condor OY-DAM operated the Copenhagen-Amsterdam-Shoreham service in April 1940.
Picture via "Illustrated Enyclopedia of Aircraft".

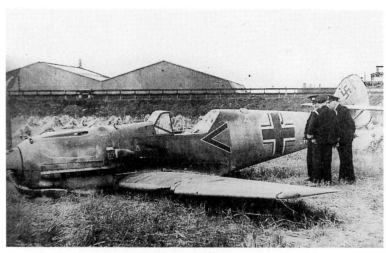

The Me. 109 which was shot down by a Hurricane on August 17th 1940, seen here in the cornfield immediately south of the airfield.
Photo: Andy Saunders.

A Westland Lysander similar to the type flown by No. 277 Squadron in early air sea rescue operations.
Photo: Westland Aircraft.

No. 277 Squadron aircrew with a Boulton Paul Defiant in 1942.
Photo: The Shoreham Airport Collection.

Aircrew of the Walrus ("Shagbats") amphibians of No. 277 Squadron, C Flight:
Cec Walker, "Dizzy" Seales and "Deky" Dekyvere.
Photo: The Shoreham Airport Collection.

Bernard Sheidhauser (second from left) with his rescuers at Shoreham on November 11th
1942. Crew L to R: "Dizzy" Seales, "Deky" Dekyvere and Eddie Quick.
Photo: L. Seales.

made a very successful "tail-up" landing with his starboard mainplane badly holed, and the aileron jammed.

Shoreham became very busy with the deployment of Hurricane IIc Squadrons in the lead-up to the abortive Dieppe raid. 253 Squadron arrived first with two supporting Handley Page Harrows complete with ground crews and stores for "Exercise Tiger". Then in June came No. 3 and No. 245 Squadrons for operation "Rutter", but this was then cancelled and the Hurricanes departed again. It would seem the military were somewhat indecisive in this period leading up to the Dieppe raid. Detailed planning of the Dieppe raid was in fact carried out in the Committee Room on the first floor of the Terminal Building.

Shoreham was frequently used as a refuelling point for Spitfire Squadrons. On June 2nd 1942, ten aircraft of 131 Squadron landed for refuelling early in the day, followed by another six the same afternoon.

During July 1942 work was carried out to improve the facilities for personnel stationed at Shoreham. This included repairs to the former homes of Lancing College staff in Hoe Court which had been empty since 1940. These were then used by 2771 Squadron RAF Regiment which had been sent to Shoreham to provide airfield defence during the Dieppe raid. A new Crash Room and Medical Inspection Room were also built, but generally Shoreham lacked facilities to cope with large numbers. The kitchens in the Terminal Building were improved, and work was put in hand at Ricardo's to provide quarters for up to 200 airmen. A Mobile Canteen was presented to the Station by the Hove Junior Ladies Jewish Guild and the YMCA set up a canteen in the Terminal Building run by a Mrs Cunliffe with a team of local helpers. The Red Lion Pub was conveniently near in Old Shoreham, and Bob Firth-Kettle, the cheerful Landlord, was well known to aircrew. They made it "within bounds" by having a direct phone line from the Operations Room!

On August 12th 1942 there was a unique encounter between a 277 Lysander from Shoreham and two FW 190s which attacked it six miles off Littlehampton. The pilot, Warrant Officer Norm. Peat, put his Lysander into a series of steep "S" bends to shake off his attackers, and his air gunner, Flt. Sgt. Wirdnam, managed to get a burst from his guns into the underbelly of one of the FW 190s; moments later it dived into the sea. The other FW 190 then made off. This was to be the only FW 190 claimed by 277 during the war although others were shot down by escorts.

"Operation Jubilee" was the code name given to the Dieppe raid, and the Hurricanes of No. 3 and 245 Squadrons returned on August 14th in preparation for the operation planned for August 19th 1942.

However on the day there were problems from the outset. A couple of 245 Hurricanes collided on the ground in the pre-dawn light, and had to be abandoned. The remainder had a rendezvous with 43 Squadron over Dieppe, but they were badly shot up by ground defences, and several aircraft were lost. Those that made it back to Shoreham and elsewhere were badly mauled. Only one 245 aircraft remained serviceable after the first mission, and ground crews had to work frantically to get seven ready to return to the action by noon.

No. 3 Squadron fared rather better, and were able to refuel and re-arm, and were off again by 7.50 a.m. for another sortie. The pace at Shoreham was hectic throughout the day with Hurricanes of both Squadrons making four or five sorties each.

In the middle of that morning a damaged Boston of 266 Squadron landed, but developed a swing to port as it tried to avoid a Defiant, and crashed outside the Battle H.Q. on the northern boundary. One of the crew who had been injured earlier in combat, Flt. Lt. O.G.E. McWilliam, later died from his injuries.

Sqn. Ldr. Berry DFC, O/C No. 3 Squadron, failed to return from an afternoon sortie. A total of five pilots failed to return from "Operation Jubilee", and another two were injured. C Flight of 277 ASR Squadron successfully located another five pilots during the day, and directed launches to them. The surviving Hurricanes left Shoreham next day, and returned to their bases at Middle Wallop and Hunsdon. Three were left behind for repairs.

A 277 Squadron Walrus pilot from Shoreham, Flt. Sgt. John L. Barber, distinguished himself during the Dieppe operation when he rescued the pilot of a Spitfire within sight of the Germans. Later he was to rescue four members of an aircraft who had spent 16 hours in their dinghy. For his meritorious service he was awarded the DFM by H.M. the King on September 17th 1942.

On August 27th a Boston of 107 Squadron made a successful high-speed emergency landing with one engine out, and in his report Sqn. Ldr. S.F. Pickup noted that this was "thanks to the new extension to the runway south west".

General Liardet and staff officers inspected 2771 Squadron RAF Regiment on September 3rd, and later that month 2787 took over defence of the Station.

On October 12th a Walrus from C Flight of 277 Squadron made a daring rescue of Flt. Sgt. Cooper of 616 Squadron just four miles from the French coast. Piloted by Sgt. Fletcher, with Flt. Sgt. Roberts and Sgt. Healey as air gunners, they landed in a minefield and were under constant shelling while picking up the pilot. Both Fletcher and Healey were awarded the DFM for this exploit, and Roberts was highly commended by the AOC.

On October 31st 137 Squadron at Manston operating Westland Whirlwinds laid on a "Rhubarb" sortie led by Flt. Lt. John Van Shaik DFM. (A Rhubarb sortie usually involved pairs of aircraft at low level under cloud). However, he was hit by flak over the target and had to ditch just a few miles off the French coast. This he accomplished successfully, and got into his dinghy. However it was 3.35 p.m. before he was located, and a Shoreham Walrus piloted by P/O Tod Hilton with Flt. Sgt "Dizzy" Seales took off to pick him up. They found Van Shaik right in the middle of a German minefield, but made a successful landing cross-wind between the mines. However they overshot the dinghy, and had to turn back between the mines with just four feet clearance on either side!

They picked him up, and started a take-off run, but just ahead they spotted a mine. They had to leapfrog over it, and dropped down again the other side before becoming airborne. They then flew their customer to Hawkinge only to discover on landing that one float had been damaged on take-off, and was full of water which caused a one-wing-down landing. Tod Hilton was awarded the DFC for this rescue, and gained the ASR quite a bit of publicity.

Not all the rescues were due to enemy action. On November 11th 1942 Spitfires of 131 Squadron were returning from a tactical exercise off the French coast when they ran into dense cloud. Unfortunately in the poor visibility P/O Bernard Shiedhauer clipped the tail of a Spitfire ahead which went down and was lost. Shiedhauer himself had to bale out, having chopped about 18 inches off his blades, and was in his dinghy for well over an hour before a Walrus, flown by F/O (Deky) Dekyvere, picked him up and brought him to Shoreham. Shiedhauer returned to his Squadron, but only a week later he was shot down and captured during a Rhubarb sortie on November 18th. Later, sadly, he was murdered by the Germans during the Great Escape from Stalag Luft III in 1944; such was the tragedy of war . . .

In his book "Another Kind of Courage", Norman Franks also includes rescues by surface craft resulting from sightings, and interestingly some reports from German records revealing their side of events.

On November 25th 1942 command of Shoreham passed to the RNAS station at Ford, and in December No. 2762 RAF Regiment took over the airfield defence.

### 1943

During February 1943 the unpopular Defiants were withdrawn and replaced by Spitfire IIs. They carried full armament with slight modifications for the ASR role. Light bomb racks were fitted for smoke marker floats, and the existing flare chutes were adapted to house survival gear. This comprised a specially designed four-man dinghy in one tube, and a connected supply pack of emergency supplies in the other. Not only could the Spitfire get quickly to the search area, but it could also provide protection for the amphibians during rescues.

On the night of February 13th 1943 Shoreham was again attacked by the Luftwaffe, and over 100 incendiaries were dropped in what was one of the heaviest raids of the war. At the time a young 18 year old airman by the name of Sydney Holden was rostered on duty watch "with a lovely young blonde WAAF from Hove". He recalls the drill was for one person to be on duty watch while the other rested in the single bed provided. If Sydney had any romantic notions they were soon to be swept from his mind . . .In the early hours they had a message to say a Wellington bomber was in some sort of trouble, and might be making an emergency landing. They could not give it much help in the poor visibility due to low clouds, and of course there was no runway lighting at Shoreham. They had switched on all available lighting, and they could hear it circling above in the gloom.

However it went away, so Sydney and his WAAF relaxed, but left the lights on just in case. Then a short time later they again heard the sound of a twin-engined plane approaching, and moments later all hell broke loose as a German bomber came in from the north, dropping a stick of bombs which landed close to Lancing College and straddled the airfield. Sydney and his WAAF dived under the bed. Then they crawled out, and looking up into the sky directly overhead they could see two Molotov Cocktail breadbaskets coming down scattering fire bombs in all directions. The bombs hit the Control Tower and other buildings, and the railway line behind was soon well alight. Trains had to be stopped while all personnel were called out to fight the fires. However, despite the large number of incendiaries dropped that night, they did not do a great deal of damage. One of the HE bombs dropped in this raid also hit the YMCA Canteen at HMS King Alfred at Lancing College. (Sydney Holden still lives nearby, and at the age of 72 he is having flying lessons at Shoreham!)

Accommodation at Shoreham was still a problem. Aircrew lived in either the Officers' Mess at the Sussex Pad or in the NCOs' quarters at Ricardo's. Many airmen were billeted with local families. One such family was the Bird family who lived at 15 Mill Lane in Shoreham, and over the years the following lived with them: AC Charlie Lowson 1940, LAC Jimmy James 1941, Cpl.(later Sgt.) Les Collins (i/c MT) 1942, LAC Les Wade 1945, and LAC Webb in 1946 (at Truleigh Hill Radar Station).

Aircrew could also elect to live out, and one was Len Healey who was billeted with the Birds in 1943-44. They also had a Canadian, Flt. Lt. George Aitchison, who was at Truleigh Hill during 1944. The Bird family were involved in other ways; both mother and teenage daughter worked at the YMCA canteen at the airfield, and a young Dennis Bird was so influenced by the RAF personnel that he too eventually joined the RAF in 1949. (He rose to the rank of Squadron Leader and was the author of an article on RAF Shoreham published in the "Shoreham Herald" of August 22nd and 29th 1975. He is also the compiler of the five chapters of Part 4 in this book.)

On April 11th 1943 an RNZAF Stirling from 75 Squadron had to ditch in the sea just four miles south of Shoreham, and 277 sent off a Walrus to rendezvous with the crippled Stirling which was being escorted home by 277 Spitfires. The sea landing was carried out perfectly by the Stirling pilot, but the rescue crew in the Walrus accidentally tipped the Stirling crew out of their dinghy. All got back into the dinghy safely, except one who slipped away on his own, and a second Walrus had to be called to pick him up. This was achieved successfully, but he had a somewhat severe case of delayed shock once he was safe . . . a not uncommon occurrence.

On April 14th 1943 a 277 Walrus was intercepted by no less than 15 Bf 109s which was a very one-sided fight. The top wing was set on fire, and Pilot Officer J. Barber alighted heavily in the sea. The Walrus sank, but Barber and his companion, P/O Len Healey, managed to escape into their dinghy, and were lucky enough to be rescued within an hour by a second Walrus from

Shoreham. They were landed back at the airfield little the worse for their ordeal a short while later.

Also in April 1943 No. 7 AA Practice Camp was set up at Shoreham to train RAF Regiment gunners, and they used Lysander Flight 1631 for target-towing duties. There were around 100 trainees on the first course for Twin Brownings which began in May.

A Gunnery Trainer Dome was built near Honeyman's Hole on the northern boundary, and this example remains to this day. Other wartime defences also remain in the form of concrete gun emplacements and air raid shelters. Among the more interesting are two Pickett-Hamilton retractable gun forts. (Robin J. Brooks describes these more fully in his book "Sussex Airfields in the Second World War".)

The airfield was swarming with RAF Regiment personnel, and the Squadrons came and went after relatively short stays. For the record these are the RAF Regiment Squadrons which served at Shoreham during the war, with the periods involved:

> 2771 July to September 1942.
> 2787 September to November 1942.
> 2824 October 1942.
> 2727 June to September 1943.
> 2885 October to November 1943.
> 2831 October to November 1943.
> 2765 November 1943 to April 1944.
> 2832 April to October 1944.

(Records for the period November 1942 to May 1943 are missing.)

During 1943 additional accommodation for RAF Regiment personnel was provided in the form of Nissen huts built along the northern boundary. The Regiment's main task was defence of the airfield and they were equipped with one quadruple Vickers, two Hispano cannons and 13 twin Brownings.

On July 10th 1943 a Boeing B-17 Fortress bomber of the United States Army Air Force (USAAF) made the first emergency landing of the type at Shoreham as the radio operator, Sgt. Jones, was very ill suffering from carbon monoxide poisoning. However, the aircraft overshot on landing causing some damage, and sadly Sgt. Jones later died in hospital. The aircraft was from 410 Squadron at Rougham, and had been on a mission to Germany. The newly arrived 2727 RAF Regiment guarded the damaged Fortress until it was repaired and flown out.

In August 1943 they had some dummy Spitfires at Shoreham. These inflatable aircraft were moved around the airfields to confuse the Germans, but it is doubtful whether they really had the desired effect.

On August 26th a USAAF B-26 Marauder 134703 based at Earles Colne in Essex tried to make an emergency landing, but overshot and crash-landed about a mile away on the Downs behind Kingston-by-Sea. There were no casualties.

On September 3rd 1943 no less than three Shoreham Walruses were involved in the rescue of a 10-man crew of a B-17 forced down 57 miles off the English coast. F/O Saunders picked up four, Flt. Lt. Dekyvere three, and Sgt. Fletcher the last three. As was so often the case, one of the Walruses, flown by Fletcher, could not take off again, and had to taxi back. He finally ran out of petrol, and had to be towed home by a High Speed Launch (HSL) to complete the return to base. Sometimes a float was damaged on landing in the open sea which prevented take-off again. A crew member had to sit out on the opposite wing to balance up the aircraft while it taxied on the surface, a journey which often took many hours.

During August and September 1943 Mustangs from 231 Squadron used Shoreham for airfiring practice. Keith Lohan flew with 231 at that time, and recalls they later used Shoreham for refuelling after Rhubarb missions over France shooting up trains. Keith Lohan also remembers swerving to avoid Lancing College Chapel after take-off on occasions! (He survived the war to return to Shoreham with the London University Auxiliary Squadron Summer Camps at Shoreham in 1946-48.)

In October No. 18 Armament Practice Camp was formed, but by the end of the year it had moved to Eastchurch. The Lysander Flight 1631 was then amalgamated with 1622 Flight at Gosport, and the two Flights became 667 Squadron. The new Squadron C Flight, made up of the former 1631 Flight, then came back to Shoreham equipped with Defiants which by then had been relegated to target-towing duties.

One night in October Len Healey and Tom Fletcher had gone out in a Walrus to pick up a Typhoon pilot down near Pointe de Barfleur. As the hours went by there was no word of them, and the Bird family back in Shoreham began to fear the worst. However eventually word came they were both at Gosport, safe, but without their Walrus which had sunk after picking up their customer. All were brought safely home by an HSL.

On October 24th there was a most unusual rescue. An Avro Rota autogyro of 529 Squadron on detachment to Shoreham for calibration work experienced engine failure just off Worthing. Not only did Shoreham Spitfires go to the spot, and drop a dinghy for the pilot, but it so happened that a Shoreham Walrus, flown by "Kiwi" Saunders, was in the area and soon picked him up.

In November "Kiwi" Saunders married Becky Green from Brighton. She too worked at the airfield in the YMCA canteen and they all had a thoroughly good time at the wedding. Sadly, just a week later, Sgt. Pilot Ray Powell of 277 Squadron, who had been at the wedding, was killed while flying a "recce" with F/O Jock Chalmers over Boulogne. He was only 19; tragedy was never very far away . . .

On November 30th 1943, a Whitley BD 259 crashed some 300 yards south of the airfield, and was written off. The aircraft broke into three pieces, but the crew were uninjured.

On the same day W/O Bert Watson arrived at Shoreham from 275 ASR Squadron in Northern Ireland as a replacement for Ray Powell. He was one of many Australians serving with the RAF at that time. 277 also had personnel from New Zealand, South Africa and Canada. Bert Watson recalls that C Flight pilots at Shoreham were a versatile group, who had developed their skills flying a variety of types from Lysanders and Defiants to Spitfires and Walrus amphibians. At that time they had about five Walruses and ten Spitfires on strength.

## *1944*

In February 1944 experiments were commenced on the 03/21 runway to determine the time taken to lay a wire-mesh runway. This was a prelude to establishing Advanced Landing Grounds (ALGs) in the Normandy invasion. The new strip laid by the Pioneer Corps was 1200 yards long by 130 yards wide, and offered an all-weather strip for the first time. Some 200 Pioneer Corps personnel were employed on this task, greatly adding to the normal numbers stationed at Shoreham which were around the 400 mark.

On February 9th 1944 another B-17 Fortress landed at Shoreham without any problems, and after refuelling it took off again. However, on February 11th 1944 four more Fortresses from the 359th Squadron of the 303rd Bomb Group at Molesworth made emergency landings due to fuel shortages. Two made good landings on the short runway, but a third Fortress, B-17G 42-31314 BS-M "Scorchy", had brake-fade on the long runway and overshot. The port wing-tip smashed into the end of the Guard House at the N.W. corner of the airfield while the other wing-tip hit No. 4 gun post, and LAC Kidd, a 7 AA armourer, was caught inside. He was seriously injured with a compound fracture to the skull. The aircraft was considerably damaged with the fuselage broken in two and both wings crumpled. The tail-plane was also torn off. The Fortress pilot, First Lt. H. Dahleen and three of his crew members were also injured and taken to Southlands Hospital. (There is a rumour that the sole prisoner in the Guard House then made good his escape through the hole!) The fourth Fortress, 42-31117 BS-L "Lonesome Polecat", made a good landing on the long runway despite having two engines out.

On the 25th another Fortress made a good landing, followed almost at once by a flak-damaged B-24 Liberator which landed heavily and burst a tyre on the still incomplete wire tracking runway.

On the 28th yet another B-17 landed safely, but as a result of these landings a good deal of the wire tracking had to be relaid, and the USAAF had to be asked not to land B-17s and B-24s again unless it was an extreme emergency. After the war, Mr. Quelch, a local farmer at Hoe Court Farm, very graphically described how he had seen all these heavy bombers, some with combat damage, lined up along the perimeter. One Fortress with engine trouble remained on site for some time, while the badly damaged one was salvaged by No. 9 MU, USAAF at Horsham. The remainder took off a few days later when weather conditions were favourable with a strong S.W. wind.

The mass formations of B-17s and B-24s used to circle high over Shoreham before heading out on these raids, and as the clear skies became covered with their vapour trails it soon became completely overcast.

By 1944 rescue procedures had been refined. Ex-F/O Bert Watson, who recalls his time at Shoreham as a Spitfire pilot with 277 from November 1943 to late 1944, wrote a chapter in "Odd Bods At War" (published privately in Australia) in which he details the sequence. Three Walruses and six Spitfires would be on the line with their engines kept warm for a quick take-off. The readiness crew would be scrambled by phone, and ran to their aircraft (2 Spitfires and an amphibian Walrus or Sea Otter). Taking straight off from the apron across the grass if wind conditions permitted, they would do a quick climbing turn, and vector on the position of the downed aircraft from radio instructions. The two Spitfires would search ahead, and flew in line abreast about three hundred yards apart, each pilot searching a strip of sea below looking inwards thus covering the blind spot over the Spitfire's nose. They would carry out a square search, and when they found their "customer" smoke flares would be dropped to mark the position. A dinghy would then be released upwind of the location which ensured it would drift in the right direction. Directed by the flares the amphibian would then land, and complete the rescue. Depending on sea conditions the amphibian pilot would not necessarily land into wind, and often had to land according to the primary wave swell.

Having landed successfully the amphibian would then be taxied up to the dinghy, lowering the landing gear to act as brakes. Using a special boat-hook the crew at the forward hatch would attach a rope to the dinghy which was then passed down the side of the hull under the wing, and the downed aircrew pulled aboard at the rear hatch. The ability to air-drop the dinghy accurately was of course essential, and practice in the technique was carried out using wooden dummies on the grass airfield at Shoreham.

On March 5th 1944 the same Bert Watson (then a W/O) located a dinghy south of Bognor Regis with six injured Americans from a ditched B-24 Liberator. Sea Otters were then coming into service with 277, and one flown by F/O "Kiwi" Saunders made the rescue. However, F/O Len Healey and Sgt Green had great difficulty in getting the crew on board in heavy seas. "Kiwi" then had a struggle to get airborne with the load, but he got off eventually, and flew them to Tangmere for medical attention. The grateful Americans made them a present of their beautiful flying boots for their efforts!

Early in 1944 the Spitfire II was replaced by the Spitfire Vb. It had a reduced capacity supercharger for low level work, and a more powerful Merlin engine which gave it a much higher cruising speed. It also had clipped wings which reduced drag.

On March 12th one more Liberator landed successfully, being very short of fuel on return from ops. After refuelling it was escorted to its parent station at Ford by a 277 Spitfire.

On March 16th 1944 277 made some tricky rescues. One was in a Sea Otter flown by P/O Tom

Fletcher with F/O Len Healey and Flt. Sgt. Gregory as crew. They rescued a Spitfire pilot so close to the French coast that they had to cross the coast before turning into wind and then landing. The Germans fired salvos which exploded all round them, but apart from a bit of shrapnel which nicked Len Healey's finger, they took off unscathed, and returned safely to Shoreham where Len's finger was bandaged. Then they were off again to the Somme Estuary where a Walrus piloted by Naval Lt. D. Robinson was in trouble as he was unable to take off with five B-17 survivors. They successfully transferred some of the Americans, but Robinson still had difficulty taking off, and by the time they both got airborne fuel was running low. They just scraped back into Friston where Robinson landed on his keel, having failed to lock down his wheels! On the same day Sqn. Ldr. Brown, C.O. of 277, also rescued three other aircrew from a Fortress bringing the total rescues for the day to 14.

On March 18th "Brownie" (as the C.O. was known) pulled off a daring rescue right under the noses of the Germans in the Somme Estuary when he picked up four Americans. However he was unable to take off with the load in his Otter, and had to taxi the 76 miles home!

On March 27th a USAAF Thunderbolt landed at Shoreham with engine trouble and a burst tyre after being shot up over enemy territory. It had considerable flak damage, and oil all over the windscreen which would have made a landing very difficult.

Around this time Flights 4664 and 4657 of the Air Construction Squadron were based at Shoreham while making the ALGs at Chailey and Coolham.

The late Sqn. Ldr. Len Healey DFC, DFM, (F/O in 1944) kept a War Diary in 1944 which makes interesting reading. In a mixture of fruitless searches for missing pilots, and the more successful rescues by 277, he reveals a sense of humour in his comments. One day in March 1944 he told of how one of the ground lads requested an air test of a Walrus. The Flight Commander, Flt. Lt. Ken Creamer, thinking he was "Chief Test Pilot", grabbed his helmet, and with F/O Walker, jumped into a Walrus outside with its engine running, and lost no time in taking off. After 25 mins in the air he reported it to be fine, only to be told by the erk "Yes I know that, you took off in the wrong one!"

277 Squadron still had two Lysanders (V 9847 and V 9545) on strength for communication duties, and they also had a Tiger Moth NL 693 which was constantly in the air in a number of mixed roles. This included flights to nearby Ford where the local Pay and Administration Office was located. There were also less official activities like the "sheep patrol" when it was used to find lost sheep on the Downs for the local Land Army girls!

Early in April The Royal Aircraft Establishment from Farnborough carried out tests with a Hurricane to determine the best type of metal runway; the rolls of wire tracking or the perforated steel plate (PSP) type. It was found the rolls invariably billowed, so the PSP won favour, and the wire tracking was removed; PSP was then installed.

In April 1944 Sqn. Ldr. L.J. Brown, C.O. of 277 Squadron, moved his H.Q. from Gravesend to Shoreham. There were detachments at Martlesham, Hawkinge, Hurn and Warmwell. There was also a Vickers Warwick flight at Portreath in Cornwall. Overall command of Shoreham had been transferred to Tangmere in March.

The Sergeants' Mess was relocated from Ricardo's to New Salts Farm in 1944, and thus once more the farm was directly involved with flying at Shoreham.

On April 26th 1944 No. 345 (Free French) Squadron arrived at Shoreham from Ayr with Spitfire Vbs. They occupied the two Over Blister hangars at the northern end of the airfield, and began an air-firing course. However, shortly after on April 29th there was a tragic crash. Sgt. Ernest Sente tried to go round again after a faulty approach, and crashed his Spitfire into a gunpost. He died later that day from his injuries.

345 Squadron was made up of personnel from a variety of backgrounds, and many had escaped from France to join the Free French forces. One of them was Charles Lagalisse. He had

begun his escape from France in March 1943 to avoid being sent to forced labour camps in Germany, and had many adventures on the way to freedom. Many young men had gathered at the French/Spanish border, and it was there that Charles met Serge Massieu. The two were to become life-long friends. To cross the border into Spain, they had to employ "guides" who demanded payment in any form . . . watches, rings and even clothes, including shoes! Avoiding the German patrols, they climbed over the Pyrenees into Spain, only to be arrested and thrown into a Spanish internment camp! Conditions in the camp were terrible and food was short. On two occasions Charles was stabbed by Arabs who tried to steal his bread ration. First aid consisted of a needle put in alcohol and stitched with thread! Eventually they were released through the Red Cross in November 1943, and made their way to North Africa, via Gibraltar. There they joined the Free French Forces and finally came to England aboard the Strathmore early in 1944.

They then joined 345 Squadron at Ayr in Scotland, and a short time later the Squadron came to Shoreham. When the Commanding Officer found out Charles Lagalisse came from a family with a gastronomic background (his father owned a restaurant in the Côte d'Or, and there was also a family vineyard on the slopes of Gévery Chambertin), he was placed in the Officers' Mess at the Sussex Pad. His companion, Serge Massieu, found himself working on the Squadron Spitfires just across the road.

On May 1st, Lord Trenchard, often referred to as the "Father of the RAF", inspected both 277 and 345 Squadrons, and "made one of his charming speeches". This was a period of many visits by V.I.P.s to Shoreham which included AVM Saunders AOC 11 Group, Group Captain "Paddy" Crisham, Sector Commander, and Wing Commander Kingaby from the Friston Wing; also the Commander of the Free French Forces in Britain, Gen. de l'Armée P.J .Koenig.

345 Squadron started operations on May 2nd with defensive patrols along the south coast, but on May 12th they began to escort Free French Bostons of 342 Squadron on sorties over France.

On May 3rd F/O "Kiwi" Saunders took off in an Otter with Flt. Sgt. Green and Sgt. Shaw as crew to pick up a Canadian pilot in the water 12 miles off Le Treport. They made a nice landing in heavy seas, but after picking up their customer they were unable to take off again. So they began to taxi back, but the Otter was taking on water in the heavy seas, and an HSL had to be called in around midnight to rescue them. Shortly afterwards the Otter sank.

During the next three months the activity at Shoreham reached its highest peak of the war with both 277 and 345 Squadron aircraft constantly in the air. With the approach of D-Day, nearby Shoreham harbour was crammed full with landing barges and troops awaiting embarkation.

By the end of May 277 Squadron had achieved 498 rescues, and there was keen competition between the three flights at Hawkinge, Martlesham and Shoreham to achieve the 500. More rescues were eagerly awaited. May 27th 1944 was a great day as Shoreham won when Spitfire pilots from Shoreham located two members of an American Boston crew in the sea 1 1/2 miles from Le Treport. They were then collected by Tommy Ormiston in his Otter. The Spitfire pilots, W/O Jackie Forrest and F/O J. Lloyd, split the sweepstake prize of £103. The Operation Record Book (ORB) soberly records that "the celebrations which followed did away with most of the prize money"!

On May 28th Flt. Lt. Robertson, with Len Healey and Sub/Lt. Mariner as crew, rescued a Canadian Typhoon pilot, F/O Watkins, who had been adrift in his dinghy off the French coast for six days without being spotted. He was in poor shape as all he had eaten was raw seagull flesh and could not have lasted much longer.

D-Day on June 6th 1944 was of course a peak of activity for both aircrew and ground crew at Shoreham. Two days before, Aircraftman Alfred Gitter of 277 Squadron was told to report to Squadron Leader Brown. Gitter had, he claims, an undeserved reputation for being able to scrounge anything in short supply. Standing stiffly to attention before his C.O., Gitter wondered what it was all about, but the C.O. just said "I've got a little job for you. I want you to obtain some paint brushes for us". Puzzled, Gitter asked "what kind of brushes, and in any case, couldn't they get the brushes from the stores?" However it seemed the C.O. wanted special wide brushes, and moreover no one was to know about it! "Just get as many as you can, and be back here by 22.30 hours", he said. Gitter was told he could take two men with him. So in company with Corporal Cheeseman and Curly Hale he set off, and later that night some 100 assorted brushes mysteriously disappeared from surrounding garden sheds! As it turned out they were used to paint the D-Day black and white stripes on all the aircraft before dawn!

345 Squadron flew three missions on D-Day covering the landings, and escorting tug/glider combinations. The Squadron suffered its first losses in action on these operations, and in the days which followed the initial landings. However, 277 had no calls for rescues during the day. With so many ships in the Channel help was not far away. Bert Watson still recalls the vast armada stretching as far as the eye could see, formed into a giant arrow-head pointing towards Normandy.

On June 10th 1944 a Walrus was delivered to Shoreham by an Air Transport Auxiliary (ATA) pilot, Flight Captain Philippa Bennett, and she made a perfect landing apart from the fact that she forgot to put the wheels down! However she hardly scratched the keel, and the Walrus was quickly put back on its "feet", but not before 277 Squadron pilots had taken photos of themselves sitting in the grass-borne Walrus! However, it seems that officialdom did not discipline the highly embarrassed ATA pilot as there was no damage.

On June 25th 277 Squadron lost one of its new and very keen pilots when F/O O'Callaghan crashed his Spitfire into a hillside near Sherborne. He had been to Warmwell in Dorset for a search in that sector when fog came down to ground level.

A week after D-Day the Germans launched the first of their V-1 Flying Bombs against the south of England, and 277 found itself with a new role. On July 4th 1944 W/O Jackie Forrest flying a Spitfire sighted a V-1 coming in over Beachy Head. He closed with it at 350 m.p.h firing cannon and machine guns. At 300 yards his starboard cannon jammed causing the Spitfire to yaw to port. So he lost ground, and only by putting the throttle "through the gate" for emergency boost was he able to catch up, and open fire again with just his machine guns. Being only 100 yards away this time his bullets found the war-head and the V-1 exploded. He flew through the explosion which was "rather like a tiger going through a fiery circus hoop" as he put it! The Spitfire was thrown 500 ft. upwards, and he flew it gingerly back to Shoreham where he landed safely without apparent damage. He sensibly resisted the temptation to do a victory roll over the airfield. Just as well he did because his Spitfire (AD 105) had been severely stressed, and never flew again (Reproduced from "Close Encounters of a V-1 Kind" or "Grandfather's Flying Bomb" by J.A. Forrest 1994.)

It was in fact only the second time a Spitfire had shot down a V-1 Flying Bomb (or "Doodlebug" or "Buzz bomb" as they were variously described). The first went to Flt. Sgt. Rollo of the Hawkinge Flight on June 29th 1944. 277 Squadron Spitfires from Shoreham shot down another two the following day. These were not bad efforts because the Spitfire could not overhaul a V-1 in straight and level flight . . . the only tactic was to dive from above. (The later technique of flying alongside them, and tipping them over with a wing tip was used by Tempests which were faster.) In all 277 Squadron shot down five V-1s.

On July 8th Lt. Nunn and W/O Quick were in Walrus 912 doing an air search about 35 miles S.E. of Shoreham when they found a German Officer (R. Jozke) in a dinghy. They brought him back to Shoreham where it was learnt that he was the sole survivor from a He 177 bomber which had been shot down over the Seine four days previously.

On July 13th 1944 a "Doodlebug" narrowly missed hitting Lancing College Chapel, and came down in the valley just behind doing little real damage, but shattering many of the green glass panes at the east end.

Aircrew of C Flight No. 277 Squadron at Shoreham in the spring of 1943.
L to R: Bob Holland, Tom Fletcher, "Deky" Dekyvere, R.F.F. Harris, Norm Peat RCAF, F.D.
Hubbard and Johnny Barber (Norm Peat would go missing in May 1943 while serving with
243 Squadron in the Mediterranean).
Photo: Len Healey.

No. 277 Squadron personnel relaxing in front of a Spitfire Vb at Shoreham in the summer of
1944. Flight Commander Flt. Lt. Ken Creamer is just behind the large man holding on to the
propeller, "Dizzy" Seales is siting on the wing next to the Naval Officer, and F/O Len
Healey is sitting cross-legged on the ground just to the right of the man in the white shorts.
Photo: Shoreham Airport Collection.

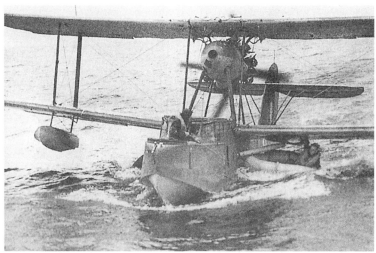

A typical rescue operation by a Walrus amphibian. Using a boat-hook and a rope the dinghy is passed under the wing to the rear hatch where the "customer" is pulled aboard.
Photo: from "Another Kind of Courage"

A Sea Otter which began to equip ASR Squadrons in early 1944. It had a much larger Mercury engine with a variable pitch propeller in the front. It even boasted an electric starter which was a vast improvement on the Walrus with its awkward hand-cranking mechanism.
Photo: R.C. Sturtivant.

No. 277 Squadron personnel at Shoreham in 1944 with a Walrus in the background. It has not been possible to identify all of the group, but in the back row on the extreme left is J.I.G. Lloyd, and Doug Robinson (Navy) and Tom Fletcher are at the right hand end. Front row: L. to R. :Flt. Sgt. Sommerville, ?/ ?/ Eddie Quick, Norm Leighton and Bill Gadd, RAAF.
Photo: Bert Watson.

Typical of the ASR activities, a returning Walrus comes to a halt by the waiting ambulance as ground crew gather round to off-load the "customers".
Photo: Bert Watson.

No. 345 Squadron Free French Spitfire Squadron at Shoreham in 1944.

Spitfire HF IX. of 345 Squadron.

Squadron hut at
Shoreham.

The two escapees from France.

Serge Massieu

Charles Lagalisse.

Photos: courtesy of June Lagalisse and
Serge Massieu.

V-Is passed over Shoreham day and night at this time, and the RAF Regiment loosed off everything they had at them. In the end they had to be restrained for fear of hitting Spitfires also trying to bring down V-1s.

During July Len Healey's family home at Watford was wrecked by a V-1 buzz bomb, and so he rented a little bungalow at Lancing for his wife Jean and their son Michael. He used to fly over it on return from ops. to let them know he was safe.

On July 14th 1944 277 was once again honoured with awards. At an Investiture held by King George VI at Tangmere three more 277 men at Shoreham received DFCs, P/O Tom Fletcher, F/O "Kiwi" Saunders, and Flt. Lt. N. Mackerith. A month later the same award went to F/O Len Healey for his part in operations off the French coast in March.

There were large number of troops stationed in the area at the time, and many were far from home, and like Charles Lagalisse could not speak English. Charles had met a local girl by the name of June Evento, and they used two Harraps dictionaries to communicate! It must have worked as they married after the war . . . There were dances every week, but June recalls one in particular on July 14th 1944, Bastille Day, when the Free French Air Force put on a huge celebration in the Dome in Brighton with French music, food and wine. There were blue, white and red flowers, and June was swept off her feet by her handsome young Frenchman. After the invasion Charles got a pilot friend of his to drop a letter over France addressed to his parents who of course had heard nothing of him since he escaped. The letter was duly delivered, to the great joy of his parents . . .

On July 23rd Flt. Lt. Dobree with W/O Birch-Hurst and Sgt. Shaw as crew found nine crew members from a USAAF bomber in a dinghy, and landed beside them in their Otter. Unable to take on board such a large number they kept station with them until an HSL came to the scene.

The battle in Normandy continued, but on July 26th there was a sudden deterioration in the weather over the beach-head, and members of 345 Free French Squadron had to make a forced landing on French soil much to their delight and emotion! After spending the night at the advanced landing ground at Bazenville, they reluntantly returned to Shoreham next day.

Meanwhile 277 was still busy picking up pilots from the sea, and by the end of July they had rescued another 60 airmen.

Around this time 277 began the task of escorting Austers across the Channel for the Army in Normandy. They flew from airfields like Bognor or Tangmere where a Walrus would rendezvous with them and act as escort. Bert Watson flew the Walrus escort on one of these trips, and recalls throttling back to around 75 knots as a gesture to the slower Austers. However, as they neared the French coast they all shot past him at 90 knots, tired of following the slow old Walrus!

On August 8th Flt. Sgt. S. Meechan was flying a replacement Typhoon to the continent when he had engine trouble and was forced to ditch in the Channel. 277 were quickly on the scene, and he was brought to Shoreham after only twenty minutes in the water. Once again the notorious Sabre engine was to blame and not enemy action!

About this time part of C Flight at Shoreham went to Warmwell to set up a new Flight. Many of the well-known names in 277 went, including people like F/O Johnny Barber, F/O Chalmers, and W/O Forrest.

Things began to wind down at Shoreham from then on as the Normandy campaign spread eastwards, and crippled bombers could land at captured airfields on the continent, thus avoiding the hazard of a Channel crossing.

On August 9th the crew of a B-25 Mitchell was rescued 35 miles off Beachy Head. Flt. Lt. Dobree landed in his Walrus and picked up two survivors, one of whom was badly hurt; so he took them to Friston.

On the same day a Sea Otter from Shoreham, piloted by Flt. Lt. Field with F/O Kennedy and Flt. Sgt. Green as crew, rescued the crew of a Dutch Mitchell 70 miles off Shoreham.

On August 14th F/O Fletcher and F/O Adams, flying 277 Spitfires, escorted another Marauder bomber in trouble and it landed safely at Shoreham.

As the need for Air Sea Rescue operations wound down there was time to relax, and the story is told of one Walrus pilot who used to land his Walrus in the Channel on calm days and do a spot of fishing to vary the Mess diet!

Then on August 16th 1944 345 Free French Squadron transferred to the ALG at Deanland near Lewes, and became part of the 141 Wing, 2nd Tactical Air Force. They were then employed on low-level attacks on road and rail targets in northern France. After a short spell at Deanland and then at Biggin Hill, 345 then went over to Belgium for the closing stages of the war.

On August 16th there was a freak accident at Shoreham involving a Spitfire of 277 Squadron. As Flt. Lt. Adams was coming into land in his Spitfire "N" Nuts, he struck a truck load of empty long-range tanks on the perimeter road and smartly wiped off his undercarriage. He was unhurt, but the Spitfire was somewhat the worse for wear.

On September 18th there was a further landing accident involving a Spitfire. W/O Bill Gadd, another of the Australians serving with 277, had the misfortune to hit a passing train as he was approaching to land. It appears his view of the train was obscured by the wing as he banked before landing, and the Spitfire hit the roof of the train taking off the aircraft's undercarriage. However, Bill Gadd made a safe belly-landing on the airfield without injury, and nobody on the train was hurt.

On September 15th the second pre-production Miles M.38/II Messenger Mk. 1 RG 333 landed at Shoreham en route to Brussels via Amiens. It was flown by Flt. Lt. T.J. Martin on a delivery flight from Woodley, and was destined to be used by Field Marshall Montgomery in Europe. Montgomery first flew in this Messenger the following day, and it was used by him until written off in a crash at Oldenburg in Germany on August 22nd 1945. Sir Winston Churchill also used the same aircraft to view the German defences across the Rhine on March 25th 1945.

About this time 277 received an Oxford as an addition to the fleet, but only Bert Watson had experience on this type. So he had to do most of the initial trips, and his modest claim of 200 hours on twins was recorded in the Squadron "Line Book" for "skiteing!"(slang for boasting used in the Squadrons).

On September 21st a Dakota made an emergency landing at Shoreham on one engine. On board were the Grand Duchess of Luxembourg and her Prime Minister en route for Luxembourg which had just been liberated. After repairs, and a luncheon provided by 277 Squadron, the aircraft took off again.

On September 26th the Air Ministry Film Unit visted Shoreham and made a documentary film using 277 Squadron aircraft. This featured dinghy-dropping amongst other aspects of ASR activities. This was not the first time Shoreham had been used for making films during the war. In 1943 Johnny Barber and Eddie Quick were featured in sequences of the film "For Those In Peril" with shots of a Walrus taking off from Shoreham. (Bert Watson has donated a video of this film to The Shoreham Airport Collection and also his own very interesting film describing ASR rescues from Shoreham in 1944.) Soon after the filming finished, 277 Squadron moved its H.Q. to Hawkinge and staff levels at Shoreham were reduced. By October all the Spitfires, Walruses and Otters had gone to Warmwell or Hawkinge, and things became quiet at Shoreham; it was placed on a care and maintenance basis for the remainder of the war.

## *1945*

On January 15th 1945 Tangmere became the Central Fighter Establishment. Spitfires of 451 RAAF Squadron were based at Tangmere and were sent on detachment to other airfields in the area. They were known to have been at Hawkinge during February and March 1945, and the occasional landings by Spitfires at Shoreham in this period may have been 451 Squadron aircraft.

According to Air Ministry records, between March 1945 and February 1946 Shoreham was a satellite of RAF Nether Wallop, but it was little used.

Sadly, in the closing stages of its history, 277 lost two of its members who had flown from Shoreham. "Robbie" Robertson and Cec Walker went missing in a Walrus during a sortie from Hawkinge early in 1945.

277 Squadron was finally disbanded at Hawkinge in February 1945 having achieved 598 rescues, and C Flight at Shoreham was the top-scoring flight. Although not really a combat unit, Spitfires of 277 shot down five V-1s during 1944, plus the FW 190 shot down by the Shoreham Lysander in 1942. Five aircrew were lost on active service. Squadron members earned many awards including 1 OBE, 12 DFCs, 6 DFMs, 1 Bar to DFM, plus American, Polish and Norwegian awards (see "Another Kind of Courage").

Although the RAF personnel had left the scene, some of them made firm links with Shoreham. Both "Kiwi" Saunders of 277 Squadron and Charles Lagalisse of 345 Squadron had married local girls, and they would retain ties with the area.

Len Healey continued to serve with the peacetime RAF, and at one time in the Middle East he found himself at the same Station as Sqn. Ldr. Dennis Bird (son of the Bird family he lodged with during the war).

After leaving the RNZAF "Kiwi" Saunders went to Rhodesia where he obtained his Private Pilot's Licence (PPL). In 1964 he returned to Shoreham and ran the Southwick garage. He also became a member of the re-born Southern Aero Club and flew many hours with Cecil Pashley.

Charles Lagalisse came back to England in February 1946, after a frustrating period when he was treated as an alien despite his war service in England! Then after marrying June Evento, he went on to a career in catering, becoming the Head Chef for Edlins Hotels in Brighton. In 1957 he migrated to Canada where he was Head Chef for The Royal Bank in Montreal. He had a marked love for the area round Shoreham, and after his death his ashes were scattered in the valley below Lancing College following a memorial service in the Chapel in 1995.

"Dizzy" Seales also settled in the area, and still lives at Shoreham Beach. In 1988 he was unlucky enough to lose a leg as the result of a road accident, but this still did not prevent him from "wing-walking" on a "Cadbury's Crunchie Flying Circus" Boeing Stearman at Shoreham in August 1995; not bad at 84!

# Chapter 6   HEALING THE WOUNDS OF WAR (1945–1950)

The war in Europe ended on May 8th 1945, and soon afterwards Lancing College boys returned from Shropshire to find just an empty airfield with no planes, and still in its wartime garb. The only activity was a detachment of the RAF Regiment detonating land mines laid around the airfield boundaries in 1940 as anti-invasion measures.

Nevertheless the airfield still attracted the interest of boys at Lancing College just as it had other boys in the past, and because it was there empty and inviting, and out of bounds. So it was after the RAF Regiment had departed that the author, then a boy at Lancing, entered the airfield with a companion called Peter Gass, and climbed into the deserted Control Tower. There they found a treasure trove left just as it was by the RAF. The operations board was still there, and they could almost hear the RT chatter in the eerie silence. Having spent a glorious 20 minutes in the Tower they made their way back, but not before taking a large wall map of the airfield. They had almost reached the airfield boundary when they were caught by the lone airfield caretaker. Names were taken, but the precious map remained undetected. However next day the pair were summoned to the Head Master's Office. Unlike his predecessors the Head Master, Frank Doherty, did not birch them or threaten them with expulsion, but he did admonish them for breaking bounds.

Although the airfield was empty, some flying did take place there in 1945. The local Air Training Corps (ATC) did some gliding at weekends using Slingsby Cadet Mk. 1s, and some two-seaters for dual instruction. A winch-equipped vehicle was used for launching their five minute flights. However, for most of the time sheep grazed undisturbed on Shoreham's grass.

The new era of jet aircraft was just begining and the author clearly remembers seeing his first RAF Meteor I jet fighter passing overhead, leaving the characteristic smoky trail of those early models.

## *1946*

On March 12th 1946 Shoreham was handed back to civil flying under the control of the Ministry of Civil Aviation. Nothing much happened until one day in May a gang mower was seen cutting the grass.

Then a few days later a lone Auster 1 (or a Taylorcraft Plus D to give the full civilian title) registered G-AHCI was seen making a circuit after approaching from the north. With mounting excitement the boys at Lancing College watched as it made one more circuit of the airfield, and then after making a low pass to scatter the sheep, it came in and landed. The pilot was none other than Cecil Pashley back from the war!

The Auster was painted in the pre-war colours of the South Coast Flying Club (SCFC), and Pashley lost no time in commencing circuits and bumps round the old familar circuit. Within a week another plane arrived. This time it was the prototype Miles Gemini G-AGUS piloted by George Miles who had flown down from Woodley.

Thus began the post-war recovery, slowly at first with a trickle of visiting planes which included Percival Proctors, Tiger Moths and Austers. In due course things picked up, and "Pash" resumed his role as CFI with an increasing band of new generation pilots. Tiger Moth G-ADIA augmented the SCFC Auster.

Privately owned aircraft began taking up residence including the Hawk Major G-ADCV, Auster J/1 G-AHHW & Proctor 1 G-AHNA.

One day a few weeks later another of Lancing College's former pupils, the late Jeffrey Quill, arrived over Shoreham in a Vampire 1 jet fighter, and proceeded to do some high-speed passes over the College. The author clearly remembers Frank Doherty, the Head Master, trying to teach Latin to a class which was distinctly distracted! For five minutes Jeffrey Quill held up everything at the College while he did a series of rolls and loops overhead before departing with an earsplitting roar! (Jeffrey Quill OBE, AFC was the Chief Test Pilot for Vickers, and did the test flights on the prototype Spitfire.)

On June 29th 1946 an Air Display was put on at Shoreham to mark the official re-opening. The airfield still looked in a mess with bombed remains of the hangars, and the Terminal Building still in its war-time green paint. However the first peace-time Air Display attracted a large crowd. Visiting aircraft included a Messenger 3 G-AGOY, Auster J/1 Autocrats G-AGVM & G-AGYI and an RAF Auster 4 NJ 629. Miles Aircraft were represented by their Gemini prototype G-AGUS. Pashley of course opened the display flying the Hawk Major G-ADCV, doing some aerobatics and executing a very low loop which surely would have ended in the ground, but he skilfully rolled off the top. George Miles demonstrated the beautiful new Gemini, and the show highlight was three Vampire 1s from RNAS Ford. They came in from the west at a very low altitude, and then shot up overhead to perform a stunning aerobatic routine. Many of the crowd had not seen jets close-up before, and the scream of the Goblin jet engines frightened some children. A local newspaper reporter described them "like the sound of 10,000 kettles"!

Then in August 1946 the RAF returned to Shoreham in the form of the London University Auxiliary Squadron which set up their summer camp. The C.O. was none other than Flt. Lt. Keith Lohan who had flown 231 Squadron Mustangs on air-firing practice at Shoreham in 1943! In 1946 the University Auxiliary Squadron (UAS) equipment was the Tiger Moth, but they really returned Shoreham to a place of great activity for a while. In addition to endless circuits and bumps all day long, the Tiger Moths were in the air at night using a kerosene flare-path for landings. Even the two lights on the Lancing College Chapel roof glowed red again. (These were removed some years later when the cost of maintaining them could not be justfied.)

By August the SCFC had taken delivery of its third aircraft, a Tiger Moth G-AHMM, and a Moth Minor G-AFNJ had been added to the private fleet.

In September 1946 Shoreham had a larger than normal visitor. The Bristol Wayfarer demonstrator G-AHJC landed on a proving flight for the Ministry of Civil Aviation. A number of take-offs and landings were completed satisfactorily.

In the summer of 1946 the World Air Speed Record stood at only 605 m.p.h., and another attempt was being made by specially prepared Meteor IV jet fighters based at Tangmere. The measured course was off Littlehampton, and the Meteors would commence their run off the coast at Shoreham, gaining speed in a shallow dive. Success came on September 7th 1946 when Grp. Cpt. E.M. Donaldson raised the speed record to 616 m.p.h.

One of the instructors who joined the SCFC at Shoreham about this time was Roy Parker who had flown Spitfires during the war. Roy had in fact landed his Spitfire VII at Shoreham for a blower test the very day in February 1944 when all the Fortresses force-landed. Roy Parker was to remain at Shoreham as an instructor until 1947. He then went to the airlines, eventually flying Britannias and Comets.

The task of restoring the Terminal Building to its pre-war white exterior was commenced late in the year. However, the Ministry of Civil Aviation failed to develop Shoreham in the immediate post-war era, and the skeleton of the bombed hangars stayed untouched for some time. The old bogey of flooding and the lack of a tarmac runway put off potential operators. Meanwhile private companies pushed ahead to improve facilities. The wartime Over Blister hangars were made more weather-proof by building walls across the western ends.

## 1947

On the northern side of the airfield opposite the Sussex Pad a new operator moved into one of the Over Blister hangars. This was Hamilton Airways who boasted just one Auster J/1 G-AGXF. Ex-RAF Wing Commander Hamilton soon proved to be a welcome ally for the boys of Lancing College who were still not allowed on the airfield. One boy would stand guard atop the bank overlooking the airfield next to the Sussex Pad, and two others would then duck across the road into the waiting Auster which was standing by with engine ticking over. The author and others used this method most successfully to make flights until the money ran out at 10/- (50p) a flight. By contrast the Dallas R. Bretts and the Christopher Clarksons of earlier Lancing generations had to walk nearly a mile to the aerodrome hangars, but this was right at the doorstep. What is more the 1947 generation never got caught!

One of the group taking part in these illicit flights was Christopher Sprent who was later to join the RAF. He was to serve for some 38 years with a varied career flying many different types including Vampires, Canberras, Phantoms, and also the Hurricane of the Battle of Britain Memorial Flight; he eventually rose to the rank of Group Captain. In his final six years he was seconded to the Sultan of Oman's Air Force as the Director of Plans and Policy. However Chris Sprent very nearly lost his life as a civilian pilot in 1989. He was involved in a mid-air collision when climbing out of Wycombe Air Park at about 100 feet, and was hit from behind by an inexperienced pilot. Amazingly all survived the resulting crash although Chris now has metal reinforcing in his left arm and leg.

Early in 1947 another Auster G-AJRJ had come to Shoreham. Its owner, John Collins, was a tea planter from Assam, and decided to buy the plane whilst on leave in England although at that stage he had not learnt to fly! Roy Parker was his instructor. It was planned for John Collins to get his licence, and then fly the plane back to Assam. Time was limited, but he got his licence, and he made many trips around the country to build up his experience. He was also cleared to fly other types such as the Proctor G-AHNA. He finally left for Assam on November 13th 1947, and successfully reached Assam early in December without incident.

February 1947 was bitterly cold and much of Britain was under snow. The airfield was covered in thick snow, and one of the very few arrivals for the month was an amphibious Ryan Seabee on its way to the continent. The pilot hade a hasty landing at Shoreham in a snowstorm on February 6th and the aircraft remained snowbound for three weeks. The author particularly remembers the period at Lancing College. One morning, after a severe blizzard during the night, he awoke to find snow had been driven through the ill-fitting windows and was in a line across the beds in the dormitory which was unheated!

On the evening of May 6th 1947 a four-engined Halifax freighter G-AIOI force-landed at Shoreham with engine trouble. It belonged to Bond Air Services and was inbound to Gatwick with a load of bananas. Fortunately the airfield was quite dry at the time and the landing was made without difficulty. The Halifax remained at the airfield overnight, and after repairs it took off from the south-west corner lifting off quite comfortably halfway across the field. A minute later it returned to make a low level beat-up across the airfield before heading for Gatwick.

On June 28th a Tea Patrol was arranged to celebrate the first anniversary of the re-opening of the South Coast Flying Club. The list of visiting aircraft included the following: Dragon Rapide G-AJHO, Auster J/4 G-AIPJ, Auster J/1s G-AGYM, G-AHCP, G-AJEO & G-AJIN, an Auster 5 G-AJFI, Tiger Moths G-AHLB, G-AIDS & G-AJOA, Proctor 1 G-AIWA, Proctor 4 G-AJMV, Globe Swift G-AHWH and a Canadian-registered Chipmunk CF-DIO-X (one of two prototypes built in Canada.)

The London University Auxiliary Squadron returned again for their summer camp in July. Once more the air was full of Tiger Moths and the sound of Gipsy Major engines. However that year there was a different sound. Three Harvards with their distinctive noisy propellers were added to the UAS fleet, "something a bit more sexy than the D.H. 82As!", as Keith Lohan put it.

Brooklands Aviation had an immaculate D.H .89A Rapide G-AKSH in full Brooklands livery, and it was a frequent visitor to the airfield that summer. A new Auster J/1 G-AJRB was added to the SCFC fleet, and other resident aircraft included Auster J/1s G-AJRJ & G-AGXF, Moth Minor G-AFPO, Whitney Straight G-AFZY, Tiger Moths G-ADIJ & G-AIDD and the Proctor 1 G-AHNA.

Members of the Lancing College Aeroplane Spotters Club, summer 1946.
The author is holding the large twin-engined model on the left, and just behind him are
(L to R): I. Hawson and R.L.T. Polgreen. Christopher Sprent is fourth from the right, and
Lawrence Williams is holding the model Auster on the left of the front row.
Photo: Author.

The Bristol Wayfarer G-AHJC which visited Shoreham in September 1946.
Photo: Author.

The Terminal Building after restoration early in 1947. Note the shadow of the yet to be restored main hangars on the left wall.
All photos: Author.

Chris Sprent of Lancing College (one of the illegal joyriders) and Auster G-AJAS, July 1947.

Brooklands Aviation D.H. 89A Rapide G-AKSH in full black, red and silver livery at Shoreham in the summer of 1947.

Interesting war relics still to be seen around the airfield boundaries at this time included the centre fuselage section of a Horsa glider TL 675 just off New Salts Farm Road.

On October 6th 1947 a Percival Gull Four G-ADOE crashed into the sea off Worthing. The wreckage was subsequently brought to Shoreham, and finally burnt on December 28th, a sad end.

While Shoreham was regaining a bit of its former glory two of its previous identities, Fred and George Miles, were in deep trouble with their company Miles Aircraft Ltd. at Woodley near Reading. They had become a major aircraft manufacturer during the war employing some six thousand people, and produced famous planes like the Magister and the Master. However their attempts to enter the post-war market with their very promising types like the Messenger, Gemini, Aerovan and the Marathon airliner, ended in financial disaster despite all efforts. FG and George were forced to resign, and the bankruptcy receiver sold the aviation assets to Handley Page who then completed production of the remaining Geminis and Marathon airliners. It was a bitter blow for them, but they would survive the disaster to set up again.

## 1948

1948 was the year the Brookside Flying Group was established at Shoreham by L.J. "Benjy" Benjamin and it operated from one of the Over Blister hangars on the northern boundary which had been used by 345 Free French Spitfire Squadron in 1944. The old Squadron Flight hut still with its wartime operations board etc. became the Club house. "Benjy" recalls that an ancient dusty red Ballot racing car was in the hangar; no doubt it was once the property of a member of 345 Squadron.

Brookside was a non-profit Community Flying Group, and commenced operations in May of 1948 with just one Miles Magister G-AKRJ which they bought from Rollasons. They had 30 flying members who paid just 30 shillings an hour to fly, and a once-only £10 joining fee entitling them to part-ownership of the Magister. Sadly they lost this when it crashed into the sea off Shoreham on January 29th 1949 and both the pilot, Bert Pitcher, and his passenger, Frank Denton, lost their lives. Despite this tragedy they soldiered on and bought a replacement Magister G-AKRM formerly owned by their neighbours Hamilton Airways. They continued flying for about another two years.

Operations at Shoreham in those days were much freer, and some of the bravado of pre-war still flying existed. As "Benjy" says, "nowadays one has to get clearance even to taxi, let alone fly!" However "Benjy" admits that his log book reveals some fairly unorthodox methods of gaining publicity, like dropping pamphlets from the air over Brighton! The pamphlets carried the message "DON'T GAZE UP AND SIGH, JOIN OUR GROUP AND FLY"!

This history would not be complete without mentioning one of Shoreham's most colourful characters, Captain H. Duncan Davis AFC, better known as "Drunken Davis". He was associated with the SCFC from its inception in 1936. Irrepressible and cheerful, he certainly enjoyed a drink or two . . . and his career was full of funny incidents. "Benjy" Benjamin recalls that one evening Drunken Davis had been drinking in the Club, and he wanted to take two pretty girls flying in the Club Proctor sitting outside. In despair the Club Manager shot out ahead of him, and got the engineer to insert a piece of paper between the contacts. "That will never start", the engineer muttered. So no attempt was made to stop Davis and his giggling passengers from climbing aboard, and when Duncan called "Clear" bystanders smiled knowingly. To their horror the engine roared to life, and Drunken Davis and his two passengers were off before anyone could react. Onlookers watched white-faced and tense, but happily Drunken Davis landed safe and sound with his shaken passengers. Drunk or sober he could certainly fly . . .

During 1948 other events were occurring which would in time impact on Shoreham. In December 1948 Miles set up a new company which he called F.G. Miles Ltd. at Redhill where he rented just one hangar. With a small band of faithful workers he did aircraft servicing and repairs. One of the staff to come from Woodley to Redhill at that time was Bert Hart. As related in Part 2, he had begun his career in aviation after a brief meeting with Charles Gates years before at

Portslade, and had joined Miles Aircraft in 1947. Bert Hart supervised the plastics shop at Redhill, and would remain with F.G. Miles Ltd. for many years in their composites work at Shoreham.

George Miles on the other hand went to Airspeeds at Christchurch as their Chief Designer. Later Grahame Gates, nephew of Charles Gates, also went to Airspeeds as a stressman. As mentioned earlier, he had joined Miles Aircraft in 1942 as a weights engineer and was later an aerodynamicist.

The London University Auxiliary Squadron used Shoreham again for their summer camps both in 1948 and 1949, and added much activity to the airfield during their stays.

The Yorkshire Aeroplane Club made a flying visit to Brighton during September, and landed at Shoreham with their fleet of three Auster J/1s, G-AGVI, G-AIGG & G-AJDW, a Messenger 2A G-AKIO, Proctor 1 G-AIEX and Proctor 5s G-AHWS & G-AIET.

Towards the end of the year Shoreham had two interesting visitors. On November 20th a Swiss Cessna Crane HB-UEF landed, and on Christmas Eve 1948 Shoreham once again heard the roar of a Merlin engine when Spitfire 16 SL 745 arrived.

## 1949

In the the the summer of 1949 a rally attracted a large number of visting aircraft including some interesting "old timers". Among them were a D.H. 60 Moth G-AAWO, Puss Moth G-AAZP, and the beautifully maintained B.A. Swallow G-AFHS. A trio of French Air Force Stampes provided aerobatics, and a fleet of D.H. 89A Rapides and D.H. 104 Doves provided joyrides.

Among the more interesting visitors to Shoreham that year were the following: D.H. 104 Dove G-ALTM belonging to Air Commodore Whitney Straight, RAF Dakota KN 642, Cessna C.34 Airmaster G-AEAI, Newbury Eon G-AKBC, Dakota G-AKOZ, Miles Martinet NR 407 and a Miles Master W 9056. Overseas registered aircraft included two Piper Super Cruisers VP-KFS & OO-ARM, Bonanza NC90568, Dragon Rapide EI-ADP and a Tipsy Belfair OO-TIA.

However, the highlight of visitors for the year was on September 24th 1949 when a Meteor 4 RA 426 from 43 Squadron at Tangmere made a hurried landing nearly out of fuel! Not that Shoreham stocked aviation turbine fuel at that stage, but at least a safe landing was made.

## 1950

By 1950 the number of aircraft at Shoreham had gradually increased. In addition to SCFC aircraft which now included another Auster J/1 G-AJDW, there were three examples of the Fairchild Argus, G-AJDT, G-AJXA and G-AKGW. Also the Swallow 2 G-AFHS, Messenger G-AIBD, Auster J/1 G-AJIS and a Leopard Moth G-AIYS. On the northern boundary the Brookside Magister G-AKRM was still in residence along with an Aeronca G-AEWU and an unidentified D.H. 89A Rapide. However, by this time Hamilton Airways had gone to Portsmouth.

On the May 28th 1950 there was an Air Display and 83 aircraft were recorded on the airfield. Included were 19 Tiger Moths (8 civil and 11 military), 15 Auster Autocrats, 8 military Chipmunks, 5 military Ansons plus a smattering of Proctors, Miles and de Havilland types; also a Bristol Freighter G-AIME and a Spitfire 21 LA 232. Flying displays were provided by Seafires, Meteors and an American Grumman Mallard NC2966, none of which landed.

In September 1950 the first International South Coast Air Race sponsored by the "Daily Express" took place. The course was from Bournemouth (Hurn) all along the south coast to Herne Bay in the Thames estuary. The £1000 first prize attracted many entries, and there were 76 starters. Shoreham was one of the airfields along the route, and among the many pre-war types seen were: Comper Swifts G-ABUS & G-ACTF, Chilton G-AFSV, Falcon Six G-AECC, Hirtenberg G-AGAK, Hornet Moth G-AELO, Leopard Moth G-ACLL, Two veteran D.H. 60 Moths G-AAWO and G-ABJJ, Moth Minor Coupé G-AFOJ, Miles Nighthawk G-AGWT, Percival Q. 6 G-AEYE, Puss Moth G-AAZP, Tomtit G-AFTA, Whitney Straight G-AEVL and Wicko G-AFJB.

The most interesting participant of all was the recently restored Mew Gull G-AEXF formerly owned by Alex Henshaw. The Mew Gull was hidden from the Germans in France during the war, and had been flown back to England in July of that year by the new owner, Hugh Scrope. Personal Plane Services, then at Blackbushe, had done a good restoration job and it looked magnificent. It was raced against one of its old rivals of eleven  years before, the Hawk Speed Six G-ADGP, but did not win a place.

A Marathon 2 G-AHXU and the royal blue and gold Hawker Hurricane G-AMAU "The Last of the Many" also took part. Visiting aircraft included an RAF Balliol VR 602 and a Leonides-powered Consul WX 587, along with the usual Austers, Aerovans, Geminis, Proctors and Rapides etc, and while not a participant, the Brabazon prototype G-AGPW happened to pass overhead on one of its early test flights.

Members of the Lancing College ATC at Shoreham in the summer of 1948.
Of the seven in this photo, three went on to fly with the RAF, and one went to civil aviation
as an airline pilot. From left to right they are:
J.C. Sprent (Grp. Cpt.), J.R. Thompson, I. Hawson, L.K.W. Williams (F/O),
T.S. New, R.L.T. Polgreen (Sqn. Ldr.), C.K. Bushe (Cathay Pacific).
Photo: Photonews via L.K.W. Williams.

Members of the Brookside Flying Group at Shoreham in the summer of 1948.
Left to right: Gordon Bick, Bert Pitcher, "Benjy" Benjamin (with dog), and front centre,
Derek Hooper( the names of the others were not recorded).
Photo: "Benjy" Benjamin.

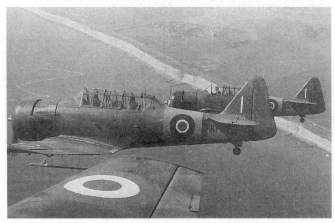

Squadron Harvards off the Sussex coast, making a turn to starboard opposite the Roedean Girls' School (still a focal point for pilots from Shoreham!). Keith Lohan is in the rear seat of KF 379, accompanying student pilot F/O Worthing.
Photo: Keith Lohan.


## LONDON UNIVERSITY AUXILIARY SQUADRON SUMMER CAMP
### JULY/AUGUST 1947

Keith Lohan on the left, with one of his senior instructors, Flt. Lt. "Trigger" Lewis.
Photo: Keith Lohan.

Looking east in 1949. In the background are the huts used by the South Coast Flying Club and the modified Over Blister hangar. All photos: Author.

The 1949 summer fly-in with a gaggle of visting aircraft. The prototype Miles Gemini G-AGUS can be seen on the right.

Visiting aircraft parked on the grass runway at the western end of the airfield. Familiar aircraft of the period are the "Flight" Gemini G-AFLT and Proctor G-AHNA. In the distance, the still-to-be-rebuilt main hangars are just visible.

Summer Fly-In 1949. Some old timers in the visitors park. From top to bottom: D.H. 60 Moth G-AAWO, D.H. Puss Moth G-AAZP and B.A. Swallow 2 G-AFHS. Photos: Author.

# Chapter 7  MILES RETURNS TO SHOREHAM (1951–1952)

## *1951*

Early in 1951 Miles entered into negotiations to lease the airfield when it became apparent the Ministry of Civil Aviation were going to withdraw and hand it back to the Joint Airport Committee.

On May 12th 1951 the Sussex Wing of the Air Training Corps organised an RAF Open Day at Shoreham with a comprehensive flying programme. Among the highlights were aerobatics by the French Lafayette Squadron, solo aerobatics by a Meteor 8 of 263 Squadron and glider aerobatics. There was formation drill by RNVR Seafires of 1832 Squadron, and No. 15 RFS at Redhill did a "Pupil and Instructor" demonstration in a Tiger Moth.

Many boys at Lancing College have been involved with Shoreham Airport over the years, but probably the most bizarre incident ever occurred during the summer of 1951. Dr. Robin Kimmerling, who was at Lancing at that time, recalls that the whole College was in the Chapel one evening singing a hymn, when their singing was rudely overwhelmed by the noise of a low-flying plane. It was so low they even caught a glimpse of it through the green glass windows as it barely cleared the roof! At Assembly next morning they learnt from the Head Master that the pilot was in fact one of their number who had decided that he would get closer to Heaven without singing hymns of praise! It appears that he had not even flown solo before, but had got into a parked plane, switched on, taxied out and calmly taken off! He had flown around perilously for about 20 minutes, and then, remarkably, had landed back at the airfield intact! However, as no damage was done the matter appears not have resulted in any legal action, and strangely no record has been kept of the boy involved . . .

On August 2nd the new owner of the Mew Gull G-AEXF, Hugh Scrope, had the misfortune to overshoot when landing at Shoreham for the the 1951 Daily Express South Coast Air Race. While he was unhurt, the Mew Gull ended up in one of those famous ditches, and suffered extensive damage which took months to repair. Hugh Scrope then found out the race had been cancelled anyway because of bad weather; he couldn't win! Grahame Gates, whose name will be recalled from earlier chapters, happened to fly into Shoreham from Christchurch aboard the Monarch G-AIDE next morning, and the Mew Gull was still stuck in the ditch.

The Daily Express race was re-staged on September 22nd and attracted 54 entries plus 38 visiting aircraft. However, that year the race began at Shoreham, not Hurn. The course followed the coast eastwards as far as Newhaven, and then swung north-east across Sussex and Kent to Reculver Towers near Herne Bay. Thereafter it followed the coastline all the way back to the finish at the West Pier, Brighton.

At the time the author was completing his Diploma course at the Chelsea College of Aeronautical Engineering (CAE) (now at Shoreham and known as Northbrook). In those days the CAE used a hangar at Redhill next door to F.G. Miles Ltd. The Redhill Flying Club Hawk Trainer G-ALFE was entered for the race, and the author was a passenger on the flights to and from Shoreham. The CAE also entered its Chilton D.W.1 G-AFSV, but neither aircraft succeeded in winning a place although they completed the course. Hugh Kendall, a former test pilot for Miles Aircraft at Woodley, won the race in the other Chilton entry, G-AFGI.

Hugh Kendall was the designer of a glider which won the 1947 British Gliding Association competition, and subsequently F.G. Miles Ltd. won a contract to build an experimental composite wing for it at Redhill, while the fuselage and tail were built at Shoreham. It was given the designation M.76, but it finally flew with wooden wings made by Elliots of Newbury.

In September 1951 two aircraft were destroyed by fire at Shoreham in mysterious circumstances. Sadly one of them was the veteran Taylorcraft Plus D G-AHCI, the very first civil aircraft to land at Shoreham after the war.

In mid-1951 Miles began his return to Shoreham with a nucleus of his design staff. On October 1st 1951 Grahame Gates arrived at Shoreham after being invited to join the team as Chief Project Designer, and in January 1952 George Miles came from Airspeed's to rejoin his brother at Shoreham. History had once more repeated itself with another member of the Gates family working at Shoreham, and the Miles brothers back where they started . . .

Grahame Gates worked directly for George Miles, and as Chief Project Designer was responsible for all new Miles projects like the conversion of the Miles M. 5 Sparrowhawk G-ADNL to the jet-powered version the M. 77 Sparrowjet, and later the Miles M. 100 Student jet trainer.

Soon after Miles returned to Shoreham in 1951 he established the Southern Aero Club (which no doubt was a reincarnation of the former pre-war Club of the same name). Brooklands Aviation and the South Coast Flying Club then disappeared.

## *1952*

Work commenced on refurbishing the main hangars in the spring of 1952. Structurally the steelwork was still sound despite the bombing as the asbestos sheeting used had merely shattered, and fallen from the steel structure. The remains of the Over Blister hangar were removed, and used to extend the one on the south-east corner. One of the Over Blister hangars on the northern boundary was no longer in use, so it too was dismantled and incorporated, thus greatly increasing the hangarage for private owners and the Southern Aero Club.

In the meantime Miles was still at Redhill doing test flights on the M. 75 Aries prototype G-35-1. One day he taxied in with a puzzled look on his face. "Something feels odd with the elevators", he said. He walked round to the tail to find half the elevator had shed in flight! Miles had used up another of his nine lives . . .

The CAE had a close working relationship with F.G. Miles Ltd. at Redhill. Ian Forbes, Miles test pilot at Redhill, took a keen interest in the activities of students. The sole remaining example of a Robinson Redwing G-ABNX was restored to flying condition by the students as an exercise, and Ian Forbes took it up on its first flight. In 1992 the author was thrilled to find the same Redwing at Shoreham with John Pothecary of Air South!

For some years the CAE had used an old RAF Tiger Moth as an instructional airframe, but in 1952 this was then made airworthy as an exercise, and became G-AMNN. It was used as a hack aircraft for the College, and the author was the passenger when it was flown down to Shoreham on its first cross-country later that year.

The refurbished main hangars were completed just before the 1952 Daily Express South Coast Air Race on August 2nd. The author came to Shoreham for the occasion, and was assisting on preparation work on one of the entrants, a Proctor, just outside the main hangars. Rain had delayed the start, and we had to push the aircraft inside for cover. As we passed the portal someone remarked that this was the first plane inside the new hangars. This was indeed so, as it was completely empty save for builders' rubbish. In a matter of minutes several other aircraft had been pushed in under cover. However, the hangars were to be used by F.G. Miles Ltd. as factory space, and did not add to hangar space at Shoreham for private owners at that time. The final assembly of the M. 77 Sparrowjet would be carried out in the new hangars. At that stage parts had already been made at Redhill.

Shoreham was again used as the start for the Race, and the 183-mile course remained unaltered. There were still quite a few pre-war aircraft taking part among the 46 entrants including two Comper Swifts, G-ABUS & G-ACTF, the Hawk Major G-ACYO, two Falcon Sixes, G-AECC & G-ADTD, the Hawk Speed Six G-ADGP, the Gull Six G-ADPR (entered by the "News of the World" and flown by Grp. Capt. Sir Douglas Bader DSO,DFC), Leopard Moth LN-TVI, Chilton G-AFGI, Moth Minors G-AFNI, G-AFOJ, & G-AFPN, Wicko G-AFJB and the Nighthawk G-AGWT. The race was won by W/C R.H. McIntosh in his Proctor 1 G-AHGA, and he describes the gruelling race in some detail in his book "All Weather Mac" mentioned earlier in Chapter 4 of Part 2.

On August 18th 1952 Grahame Gates recorded his first flight in the prototype Aries with George Miles on an airspeed calibration test.

On August 28th 1952 a Wellington T.18, NA 989, force-landed at Shoreham adding to the list of unusual visitors. At that stage not many Wellingtons were still airworthy.

The airlines returned to Shoreham during 1952 when East Anglian Flying Services started operations with flights to the Channel Islands. They used D.H. 89A Rapides on the route which included calls at Ipswich, Rochester, Southend, Shoreham and Portsmouth on the way to the Channel Islands.

Resident aircraft at Shoreham in 1952 included the Aries M. 75 prototype, by then registered G-AMDJ, Hawk Trainers G-AITS and G-AIZK owned by F.G. Miles Ltd., a Proctor 4 G-AJMH and Proctor 5 G-AHBI.

Meridian Air Maps began operations from Shoreham at this time, and they had close ties with F.G. Miles Ltd. They did aerial survey work using the Miles Aerovan G-AJKP, but sadly this aircraft was lost in 1957 in a tragic accident near Manchester, when a well-known and very experienced pilot, Jean Bird, lost her life. Meridian later operated Austers, a Consul and Avro Ansons

By this time the remaining design staff had come to Shoreham from Redhill, and operations were consolidated at one location. Bert Hart took up his job as supervisor of the composite shop at Shoreham, and the Sparrowjet project continued. Design work would soon commence on the Miles M. 100 Student jet Trainer. Jeremy Miles, son of "FG" and former Fleet Air Arm pilot, joined the company about this time and worked with Grahame Gates on the Student project.

F.G. Miles Ltd. had been investigating the use of reinforced plastics for aircraft construction, and now they proposed an all-plastic towed target of 25 feet wingspan. To test the aerodynamics Grahame Gates designed a 1/4 scale model in wood, and air tests were carried out towed behind the Aerovan 6 G-AKHF with the rear door removed. The results were most encouraging with the model showing extremely steady flying characteristics under tow.

A whole new era was about to commence at Shoreham by the end of 1952, and the next decade or so would see many changes. Aircraft manufacture would become a dominant feature.

So we come to the end of Part 3 which saw Shoreham survive the war years with all its traumas and emerge once more as a civil airfield. Shoreham has outlived other famous airfields in Sussex like Tangmere, Ford and Thorney Island, all of whom had histories going back many years. Both Tangmere and Ford began in WW I, and while Tangmere still has its Military Aviation Museum, the others have lost all traces of their past, although Thorney Island does have a memorial plaque.

Thus Shoreham has had a unique role in the history of Sussex aviation worthy of recording for posterity. However, it is sobering to realise that this history so far only covers the first 43 years, and as much again in terms of years have gone by since 1952.

Originally the author had contemplated a later edition covering the years 1953-1996, but it was felt that readers would want a more complete work from the outset. Dennis L. Bird has kindly prepared Part 4 to meet that need, and now the reader can trace events right through to 1996.

Peter G. Campbell has also written two books which complement this work. In " The Fifties Revisited" he recounts his personal experiences as one of the next generation of spotters at Lancing College in the early fifties, including his holiday job with F.G. Miles Ltd. in 1955. His later book "Shoreham Airport: a Record of Visiting Aircraft 1946-1970", is a comprehensive record of aircraft movements of the times. (Details of aircraft seen at Shoreham 1946-1952 by courtesy of Peter G. Campbell, Keith Donald, Fred Lynn and "Air Britain".)

**END OF PART 3**

The Percival Mew Gull G-AEXF seen here in fine trim just before the first "Daily Express" International South Coast Race in September 1950.

The College of Aeronautical Engineering's Chilton G-AFSV which was flown in the "Daily Express" South Coast Air Race held at Shoreham in 1951. (The author appears at the wing tip on the extreme right.)

The author with a girl friend at Shoreham in September 1951, with Redhill Flying Club Hawk Trainer G-ALFE.
All photos: Author.

The Over Blister hangar which was built under the remains of the bombed main hangars in 1941 still in use around 1949 by aircraft of the London University Auxiliary Squadron. Note the RAF Miles Magister in the foreground.
Photo: Keith Donald.

Rebuilding the Main Hangars in April 1952.
Photos: Author.

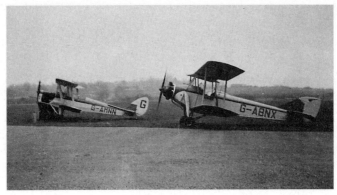

The Redwing G-ABNX seen here at Redhill with the Tiger Moth G-AMNN in the summer of 1952.
Photo: Author.

The Avro XIX G-AHKX of Meridian Air Maps at Shoreham.
Photo: "Flypast" May 1994.

An action shot of the author on his motor cycle taken at Redhill in 1952. The tail of the Aerovan G-AKHF which was captured in this view was the very same aircraft used by Grahame Gates later that year for the 1/4 scale model glider towing tests at Shoreham. Photo: Author.

# Part 4 (1953–1996)

## INTRODUCTION

*As a boy, I grew up in Shoreham before and during World War II. The Airport was a major feature of the town, and it stimulated in me a lifelong interest in aviation. I saw my first Hawker Hurricane there, at an air show in 1939. A powerful influence was our next-door neighbour, William Storm Clark (son of the novelist Margaret Storm Jameson). He was a pilot with Olley Air Services, flying D.H. Rapides from Shoreham to the Channel Islands.*

*As revealed in Chapter 5, my family had close ties with the Airport during the war. My sister and my mother worked in the YMCA canteen at the Airport, and from 1940 to 1946 RAF men were billeted on us, including the much decorated Sqn. Ldr. Len Healey. Shoreham Airport has thus played an interesting part in my life, leading to my RAF career of nearly 20 years.*

*When I heard Tim Webb was writing the history of Shoreham up to 1952, I felt some attempt should be made to carry the story forward over the next 44 years. The result is Part 4, which covers all the more important events in the period, particularly the rise and fall of Beagle Aircraft and the prolonged debate on the hard runway issue. Richard Almond's scrapbooks have provided a wealth of information, and I could not have done the job without them.*

*DENNIS L. BIRD*

## Chapter 8    THE END OF THE MILES ERA (1953-1960)

### Biro Pens

Frederick G. Miles (1903-1976) was a remarkable man, as will be evident from the foregoing pages. Nor were his interests confined solely to aviation. During his lifetime he was Chairman of Miles Nautical Instruments Ltd. and Hivolt Ltd., and during World War II he and a businessman, Henry Martin, set up the Miles-Martin Pen Company at Reading. Here 20 young women turned out 30,000 ballpoint pens to the design of the Hungarian journalist Laszlo Biro. They were of great value to RAF aircrews who could not use fountain pens at altitude as they leaked. In December 1945 the pens went on sale to the public. They were not cheap, and at 55 shillings (£2.75) each, they cost the weekly wage of a secretary. But they revolutionised the writing habits of millions, and everyday calligraphy has never been the same since.

### The Sparrowjet

However, it is with Miles' aeronautical activities at Shoreham that this book is concerned. As already related, he returned to his old haunts in 1951 as F.G. Miles Ltd.

One of their first projects was the Sparrowjet, which had an interesting and unusual history. In 1935 Miles took some standard Miles Hawk components and built the prototype Miles M.5 Sparrowhawk G-ADNL, powered by a 147 h.p. D.H. Gipsy Major engine. It was a single-seater which he flew in the King's Cup Air Race on September 7th 1935. He won the speed prize at an average of 163.64 m.p.h, but finished only 11th in the final results. The aircraft was then sold, and passed through several hands until in 1950 it was bought by a Lancashire enthusiast, Fred Dunkerley, after it had won a race round the Isle of Wight. He then had the curious idea of converting it to jet power.

In December 1950 he sent it to Miles at Redhill to be rebuilt. It was given an entirely new front fuselage and tail, and in 1952 two 330 lb. static thrust Turboméca Palas jet engines were installed at Shoreham. It was now renamed the Miles M. 77 Sparrowjet. It did not fly until December 14th 1953, when George Miles had his first experience of jet flight. It was capable of well over 200 m.p.h, but as it took some time to reach this speed, it suffered in handicapping. However, Fred

Dunkerley eventually piloted it to victory in the 1957 King's Cup race at the remarkable speed of 228 m.p.h. After 22 years it had advanced from 11th to first. In that race, Miles aircraft finished 1st, 2nd, 3rd, and 5th - a result never achieved by any other manufacturer.

The Sparrowjet was afterwards presented to the Royal Aeronautical Society. Sadly, it was destroyed in a hangar fire at RAF Upavon in July 1964. Curiously, its registration G-ADNL was re-allocated in 1992 to a Miles Sparrowhawk owned by one Kathleen Dunkerley, which suggests that some parts of the original may have survived the fire.

## The Student

Enthused by their first venture into jet flight in 1953, the Miles brothers decided to build a jet trainer, hoping to take advantage of the recent RAF decision to provide all-through jet tuition for Service pilots. This led to the Student, which was allotted the first number in a new Miles series, M. 100. The Student was a side-by-side two-seat high-wing aircraft with a tricycle undercarriage and an 880 lb. s.t. Turboméca Marboré engine. It was a private venture, and construction was delayed because of Miles' limited capital resources. It did not fly until George Miles took it up on May 14th 1957. However, it was too late; the RAF had already decided to adopt the Percival Jet Provost.

The brothers did not give up. They installed a Marboré 6F turbojet giving 20% greater thrust, and the Student II was flight tested by George on April 22nd 1964. There was some hope that it might be sold to the South African Air Force, but at that time political objections to the apartheid policies of the South African Government resulted in an embargo on exports to that country.

Other plans for a Miles Graduate four-seat communications variant and a slightly larger Centurion came to nothing.

## Hurel-Dubois

In March 1954 one of the visiting aircraft at Shoreham was the Hurel-Dubois HD-31 from Villacoublay in France. It was a strange machine with an enormous wingspan. It had been designed to investigate the possibility of reduced drag at low speeds by using a wing of very high aspect ratio. George Miles was interested and a new company was formed called "H.D. et M. (Aviation) Ltd.", a joint enterprise of F.G. Miles Ltd. and the Société de Construction des Avions Hurel-Dubois to develop the application of the Hurel-Dubois wing to a Miles aircraft. So George took one of his 1944-designed Miles Aerovans, G-AJOF, and fitted it with a Hurel-Dubois wing (aspect ratio 20.5). The Aerovan's normal wingspan of 50 feet was thus extended to 75 feet 4 inches, with a root chord of only 4 feet 7 inches. This became the one and only HDM. 105, which was subsequently allocated the highly appropriate registration G-AHDM.

Successful trials were carried out with this aircraft which led to the development of the HDM. 106, 107 and 108. The HDM. 106 Caravan was eventually sold to Shorts and developed as the Short SC-7 Skyvan, but with an aspect ratio reduced to 11 with a corresponding increase in induced drag. G-AHDM was damaged beyond repair in a landing accident at Shoreham on June 20th 1958.

## The Meteor Test-Bed Project for Rolls-Royce

One of Miles' most important projects was a contract from Rolls-Royce in July 1955. They needed a flying test-bed for the RB.108 engine which "could cover the transitional flight range between vertical take-off and level flight with the lift engines shut down," as George Miles put it in a letter to Peter Campbell in 1989. The Gloster Meteor FR.9 VZ 608, modified by Miles, provided data for the design of the Short SC-1 vertical take-off research aircraft and ultimately for the Hawker Harrier "jump jet" which formed so vital a part of the Falklands Task Force in 1982. Peter Campbell advises the Meteor VZ 608 is still in existence at the Winthorpe Air Museum in Nottinghamshire.

In his book "The Fifties Revisited" Peter Campbell recalls how the Head Master at Lancing College was persuaded, rather against his will, to let Peter do three weeks'Δ work with F.G. Miles Ltd. in July 1955. However, recognising Peter's real interest, George Miles allowed him one whole week of his "work experience" with Air Traffic Control, instead of working as a fitter's mate in the assembly sheds for the whole period. For an aviation enthusiast that was far more acceptable! Little did Peter know that 41 years later he would be the publisher of this book!

## The British Flight Manuals

As Chief Project Designer for F.G. Miles Ltd., Grahame Gates became involved in a new sphere of Miles work in 1959.

Because of the need to minimise dollar expenditure, post-war British Governments imposed restrictions on imports from the USA. In 1959 these restrictions were relaxed, leading to new demands for American light aircraft. However, these imports could only be sanctioned if they were in accordance with a "British Flight Manual", a document which laid down performance specifications. US manufacturers were not willing to produce the required data, and so there was a need for someone to test foreign aircraft. This looked like a suitable job for Miles, and it was undertaken by Grahame Gates. Piper and Cessna products were the aircraft types most involved.

Grahame Gates tells an amusing tale of a take-off and landing test on a Piper Apache at nearby Ford aerodrome (there being no hard runway at Shoreham at the time). The former Fleet Air Arm station had been closed and it was now an open prison, but the owner of the airfield had agreed with Miles that they could fly there occasionally. After the Apache had landed, a Jaguar car appeared, containing two police officers. They wondered why an unusual type of aeroplane should land so near one of H.M. Prisons. Could this be a rescue attempt? They took some convincing that this was a normal flight test!

The British Flight Manual programme ran from July 1959 to April 1964, and involved Miles in checks on 32 aircraft, including an elderly DHC-2 Beaver in an "incredibly scruffy" condition. These tests gave F.G. Miles Ltd. a wealth of experience for the subsequent M. 114/115 projects.

## Other Projects

The tasks carried out by F.G. Miles Ltd. were many and varied, including modifications in 1955 to the Miles Gemini flown for Shell Aviation by the legless Battle of Britain ace, Group Captain Sir Douglas Bader. He knew the area well, having been leader of the Tangmere wing of Spitfires in 1941 when he had to bale out over France and was captured.

In 1960, George Miles prepared his own designs for replacements for the Messenger and Gemini. The M. 114 was to be a cheap, simple two-seater with a 100 h.p. Rolls Royce Continental 0-200A engine; the M. 115 (later numbered M. 218) was a four-seater powered by two Continentals. He and Grahame Gates took these proposals to the Ministry of Aviation in the hope of securing Government aid. However, by now it appeared the Shoreham firm was in financial difficulties, and in November 1960 the Ministry said there would be no support unless there was a merger with a company of "better financial standing." Thus sounded the death knell of F.G. Miles Ltd.

# Chapter 9  THE BEAGLE STORY (1960-1970)

What at first looked like an ideal solution was about to emerge. But the events of the 1960s at Shoreham were so complex and unsatisfactory that it is not possible to give a detailed account here. Michael Jerram told the full story in four long articles in the monthly magazine "Pilot" in April, May, June and July 1983, and I can do no better than to summarise them.

The late 1950s were difficult times for the British aircraft industry as a whole. Big and famous companies had serious problems, and there was pressure from the Government for many of them to merge and thus lose their historic identities. The Bristol Aeroplane Company was one such, and it was swallowed up, together with Hawker Siddeley and Vickers-Armstrong (Supermarine), in the giant British Aircraft Corporation.

Bristol's managing director left the company, taking with him a bright new idea. He was Sir Peter Masefield, who twenty years earlier had endeared himself to every schoolboy as the first editor of the indispensable journal "The Aeroplane Spotter". It was published fortnightly by Temple Press from 1941 to 1948, contained no advertising, never cost more than three old pennies (less than 1½p in today's money), and it did more for the vital wartime art of aircraft recognition than any other publication before or since.

Masefield's new idea was for a company to develop two designs for light aircraft - the embryo Bristol 219 and 220. He took these plans to the Pressed Steel Company, profitable makers of car bodies for the British motor industry. Eager to diversify, they agreed, and announced on October 7th 1960 the setting up of a new subsidiary, to be called British Executive and General Aviation Ltd. The obvious acronym "Begal" was subtly altered to "Beagle" to appeal to the dog-loving British public. As Sir Peter wrote in "Flight", "Beagles are distinguished for their good manners, obedience to command, handlability, and enthusiasm". The Press immediately caught on to the canine theme, writing of "Beagle scenting for business", producing "litters" of aircraft, needing "guards for kennels". Michael Jerram adds that someone unkindly pointed out that a beagle is also a type of shark . . .

The new company was chaired by Michael Bellhouse of Pressed Steel, with Masefield as managing director. In 1961 his former BEA colleague, Peter Wright Brooks (1920-1996), joined as his deputy, and later joint managing director.

A team with design and engineering expertise was needed, so the Miles brothers were invited to join Beagle and, although they initially declined, they did contract with Beagle to design and build the B. 206X light twin prototype in time for the Farnborough SBAC show in September 1961. R.E. "Dicky" Bird was the Design Manager for that project and Grahame Gates was  Design Manager for the Miles M. 115 light twin (later to become the Beagle-Miles M. 218). The Miles brothers later agreed to transfer the aircraft portion of their company to Beagle-Miles, and control of the airport also passed to Beagle. There were now three elements to Beagle. One was Beagle-Auster at Rearsby in Leicestershire, which had taken over the company originally set up to manufacture the American Taylorcraft D (Auster). At Shoreham there was Beagle-Miles, retaining the well-known Miles name as part of their agreement. Also at Shoreham there was what was really "Beagle-Masefield", a design office led by the managing director's colleague from Bristol, Ronald Woodhams. Their specific task was to design the B. 206Y, a production version of the prototype B. 206X. The production B. 206 was then predicted to cost £20,000 and Masefield saw bright prospects for the development of Shoreham Airport, with a hard runway (this did not materialise for another 22 years) and up to 800 jobs.

## B. 206 and M. 218.

The prototype B. 206X (G-ARRM) was rolled out at Shoreham on August 15th 1961, to the acclaim of the aeronautical press, but this led to the first real difference of opinion with George Miles. A second design team had been set up, and George Miles later said "Two entirely different 206s were being designed; our 206 (the 206X which was a Cessna 310 counterpart) and the Beagle office's" (the 206Y). Design specifications for the latter were constantly being changed after discussions with the RAF, making it larger, heavier and more expensive, eventually becoming the D.H. Dove counterpart.

In 1962 relations between Beagle management and George Miles (whose brother had already left the company) were becoming increasingly tense, with George voicing his growing concern to the Beagle board of directors. The B. 206Y production prototype (G-ARXM) flew on August 12th 1962, a week before George flew his M. 218 (G-ASCK). Both flew at the Farnborough SBAC show in September 1962, at which the following specifications were quoted:

M. 218 : 4-place, 2 x 145 h.p. engines, 3200lb. gross wt., £9,000 cost.

B. 206 : 7-place, 2 x 310 h.p. engines, 7500lb. gross wt., £29,950 cost.

As can be seen, the types complemented each other, rather than rivalling each other as has sometimes been suggested. The only rivalry was for available funds!

Further friction between George Miles and Beagle management resulted from dropping "Miles" from the Beagle-Miles name, all three elements now being called "Beagle Aircraft Ltd."

## The Wallis Autogyro

At this period, Beagle at Shoreham were working with a retired RAF officer, the inventive Wing Commander Kenneth Horatio Wallis, C. Eng., FRAeS. He had come to Shoreham in January 1959 with the American Bensen gyrocopter (an autogyro rather than a helicopter). He carried out experiments on his own ideas, resulting in the first flight of his tiny Wallis WA. 116 on August 2nd 1961. Next year five more were produced for evaluation by the Army, but only one was ordered by the Ministry of Defence. The WA. 116 had more success in other ways: three of them were used used in the popular James Bond spy films, and on May 11th 1968, Wg. Cdr. Wallis set up a World Class E 3 height record of 15,220 ft - chilly work as he was almost as exposed as the pilot of a hang-glider!

Sadly one of his Wallis autogyros later crashed at Farnborough in 1970, killing the former Beagle chief test pilot, Pee-Wee Judge. However, Wg. Cdr. Wallis continued to produce new models in Norfolk where he later set up his operations, and he kept in touch with Shoreham. He flew his WA. 116 "Little Nellie" to Shoreham for the 1979 air show.

## Staff Redundancies and the Departure of the Miles Brothers

Beagle's internal problems became more acute. By the spring of 1963, a string of senior staff had resigned or had been dismissed, among them F.G. Miles himself, Ron Woodhams, and the commercial director, Sir Mark Norman (whose brother Desmond helped to produce the Britten-Norman Islander). George Miles felt that little attempt had been made to market his M. 218, and a German order for 20 from Bölkow had been rejected because it was felt it might jeopardise sales of Airedales and Terriers (Auster developments).

Eventually after much recrimination, George Miles resigned on July 8th 1963. Earlier in the year there had been 90 redundancies among technical, works and administrative staff. Another of the former Miles identities, Grahame Gates, was also becoming increasingly frustrated by the turn of events, and a year later in November of 1964 he left the scene for a job in the USA with Piper as a senior design engineer, where he later became their Director of Advanced Engineering. However, his many years' association with Shoreham, and having an uncle involved with Shoreham's early history, has ensured his continued interest in the place, and he still regularly makes visits. His contributions to this history have been invaluble.

## The Basset

The company was now pinning its hopes on selling the B. 206, later named the Basset, to the RAF, and some 20 were in fact delivered to Communications Squadrons. They were used alongside Devons, Andovers and Sycamore helicopters. One, colloquially known as the "Regal Beagle", was used by HRH Prince Charles for multi-engine training. However, in service the Basset had many failings, such as problems with the undercarriage, engine sump, cracked exhaust augmenter tubes and engine bearer vibration. Beagles hopes for an order for 90 were dashed and B. 206 production was then cut back from 250 to 50, and the work was transferred from Shoreham to Rearsby.

The type was eventually withdrawn by the RAF on the May 28th 1974 after a short service life of only nine years, and their place was taken by Devons and HS. 125s. The reasons given for their withdrawal were "poor reliability, poor hot and high performance, insufficient payload & range to transport V-bombers' crews". When the House of Commons Public Accounts Committee investigated expenditure of public money on the Basset, the chairman, John (now Lord) Boyd-Carpenter asked who had named the Basset. "This, as compared with a beagle, is heavy, slow, and feels the heat". Quite an appropriate comparision, unfortunately!

## Beagle and Financial Difficulties.

Pressed Steel, the parent company, became concerned when Beagle made a net loss of £2.1 million in 1962, and began to think of pulling out. The recession in the motor industry worsened from 1961, and now Pressed Steel themselves were in trouble. Stunned by the costs, they sought Government help for Beagle, and on February 12th 1965, the then Parliamentary Secretary to the Ministry of Aviation, John Stonehouse (later famous in another context), announced that the Government would give £600,000 towards research and development.

In July 1965, Pressed Steel were themselves taken over by the British Motor Corporation, who did not want their aviation interests. Beagle directors desperately sought a buyer, but without success. Eventually in December 1966, the then Minister of Aviation, Fred Mulley, announced the Government were buying Beagle for £1 million; the alternative would have been a close-down and a thousand redundancies.

In July 1968, Beagle was formally taken over as a wholly-owned Government company, with £4.4 million invested. The Minister of Technology, Anthony Wedgwood Benn, forecast 400 export orders by 1972 earning some £5.25 million. Sir Peter Masefield was nominated as chairman by the Government, with K.N. Myer as managing director. However, he had no background in aviation, having been recruited from Thorn Electrical. He set about a complete re-organisation, cutting staff drastically in the project design and ancillary departments. Among those who went were test pilot Ranald Porteous and Peter Masefield's former deputy, Peter Brooks. But the Government still had hopes for the company. Tony Wedgwood Benn flew to Shoreham in January 1969, symbolically in a Beagle B. 206, to re-affirm to the Shoreham workforce the Government's intention to continue its support.

## The Pup and the Bulldog

Reprieved, the Shoreham design team produced the B. 121 Pup with a 100 h.p. Rolls-Royce Continental engine. It was an all-metal two-seat aerobatic machine, worthy to follow such trainers as the classic Avro 504K and D.H. 82A Tiger Moth. It was first flown on April 8th 1967, by Pee-Wee Judge, Beagle's chief test pilot, and on May 17th it was formally named in a ceremony at Shoreham by the 89-year-old pioneer airman, Sir Tom Sopwith (1888-1989). Alongside the Beagle Pup that day was the sole surviving Sopwith Pup of World War I vintage, from the Shuttleworth collection (illustrated in Part 2).

It was soon obvious that the Beagle Pup was a first class aeroplane. Among those who flew it with satisfaction were the Duke of Edinburgh and the veteran airline pilot Captain O.P. Jones. In December of 1967, the Ministry of Aviation signed a contract for a new Pup assembly building at Shoreham. Soon there were 250 orders for the little trainer, and in 1968 four were delivered to Frank Hewitt's Shoreham School of Flying. Others went to Miami Aviation, the Iranian Civil Air Training Organisation, and purchasers in Australia, Austria, Finland, Malaysia, Sweden, Switzerland and elsewhere, as well as to flying clubs in the British Isles. Soon Pup production accelerated to one a day. A total of 168 were built, most of them at Shoreham and a few at the Auster works at Rearsby. Eight unfinished airframes were later completed at Elstree.

On April 1st 1969 the prototype Pup flew with the doubled power of a 200 h.p. Lycoming engine. This led to the development of the Bulldog as a military trainer. The Swedish Air Force ordered 58, the Royal Malaysian Air Force 15, and eventually the RAF wanted 130.

## The End of Beagle Aircraft Ltd.

However, despite this sudden success, all was not well with Beagle. In late 1969 the Shoreham School of Flying announced they were selling their fleet of Pups because of Beagle's "poor response to fault rectification". The Government were also once again becoming worried about the financial position at Beagle. In October 1969, Sir Peter Masefield, K.N. Myer, and the Government-appointed financial director, T.N. Ritchie, met Wedgwood Benn and his deputy, Harold (later Lord) Lever at the Ministry of Technology, seeking a further £6 million of Treasury aid. Two months later the Minister told the House of Commons that "there is not sufficient priority to justify the investment of further public funds."

On February 20th 1970, at an Extra-Ordinary General Meeting of the Beagle company, Kenneth Cork was appointed as Receiver. He valued the assets at £1.2 million, and a buyer was sought. The Miles brothers made a last attempt to return to Shoreham Airport, but their bid was not accepted; Miles Aviation and Transport Ltd. had offered "well under £400,000" for the Bulldog sub-contract work. Colin Chapman of the Lotus motor-racing firm was interested; so were Messerschmitt-Blohm in Germany, but nothing resulted. By March only 250 staff were left. Eventually C.F. Taylor Holdings bought Beagle Aircraft (1969) and transferred to Christchurch as a supplier of aerospace assemblies. In June 1970, Scottish Aviation at Prestwick, Glasgow, took over the Bulldog export orders and the RAF contract. So sadly came the end of the Beagle saga and aircraft construction at Shoreham (for the third time in its long history).

While the future of the Pup and the Bulldog would have appeared uncertain at that stage, an article by Ken Ellis entitled "School for Dog Handlers" ("Flypast" February 1966) revealed that both the Pup and the Bulldog have since earned a place in the history of air racing. A Pup took the winning place in the Schneider Trophy of 1986 and the King's Cup in 1989. In 1994 Roger Hayes won the King's Cup in a Bulldog (or "Dog" as they have become known). Some 60 plus Pups are on the British register and an increasing number of ex-military Bulldogs are appearing. This has led to the formation of two groups of Beagle Pup/Bulldog enthusiasts; the Beagle Pup Club was formed by Roger Hayes and Terry Hiscock in 1984 and more recently Skysport was formed in 1994. So although the original concept for the Pup series came from George Miles' Miles M.114 design at Shoreham in 1962, the type lives on and is now regarded as a much sought after classic aeroplane (Ken Ellis is Contributing Editor for "Flypast").

## Miles-Dufon Air Services Ltd. and Miles Engineering Ltd.

After their split with Beagle the Miles brothers set up some new business enterprises. Miles-Dufon was one and operated as a sub-contractor for the Short SD.3-30. Another was Miles Engineering which had a highly unusual historical task in 1964. They were commissioned to build a replica of the 1910 Bristol Boxkite to be used in that classic of films "Those Magnificent Men in their Flying Machines," and George Miles made the first flight from Ford airfield on May 6th 1964.

Miles Engineering were also commissioned to build other replicas, and in 1967 they built two replica S.E.5As, G-ATGV and G-ATGW, for the film "The Blue Max."

# Chapter 10    A MUNICIPAL AIRPORT AGAIN (1971)

On May 15th 1971 Shoreham once again came under the control of the Joint Municipal Airport Committee and was re-instated as the Brighton, Hove and Worthing Municipal Airport. A former marketing manager of Beagle Aircraft Ltd., Ben Gunn, was appointed as the new airfield manager.

The Airport has had a chequered career, and at times there were doubts about its continued existence. Its problems have been manifold: an often water-logged airfield, the collapse of some tenant companies, controversies over noise and the need for a hard runway. The airport has rarely made a profit over the last 25 years. In 1970/71 there was a modest surplus of £7,918; in 1989/90 it was £23,549, but in other years the deficits have ranged from £16,863 in 1973/74 to £148,477 in 1983/84 and £128,185 in 1991/92. However, air movements have grown dramatically: 8,530 in 1954 to 34,539 in 1972, and to 76,000 in 1989. This has led to more profitable results in recent years, and in 1993/94 the profit was £40,000. While there is a history of deficits made up by the three local authorities, if the returns continue at current rates this could be wiped out over the next three to four years.

## Scheduled Services

Over the years more than 30 airline companies have tried to operate profitable routes to the Channel Islands and the continent with varying degrees of success. As mentioned earlier in Chapter 7, East Anglian Flying Services (later Channel Airways) commenced operations with a service to the Channel Islands in 1952. The staff included the first fully-qualified woman airline pilot in Britain, Jackie Moggridge, of wartime ATA fame. Initially they employed four D.H. 89A Rapides, but by 1955 they were also using three D.H. 104 Doves. In later years Douglas D.C.3 Dakotas were used until they ceased operations at Shoreham in 1961.

After the Beagle collapse in 1970, John Fisher Airlines (JFA) of Portsmouth re-started services to the Channel Islands using Twin Pioneers in 1972. Later they used Britten-Norman Islanders and Trislanders, but sold out to Jersey Ferry Airlines, who only lasted two years.

Then came Haywards Aviation in 1977 with Piper Aztecs, and they also flew to Dieppe. Aurigny Air Services started the following year with Islanders, and in 1979 offered a service to Alderney. In 1980 another rival appeared; Jersey European Airways, who later merged with Haywards in 1981. They flew 20-seat D.H. Canada D.H.C-6 Twin Otters, and despite extending their services to the island of Guernsey and other destinations on the continent, they never made a profit and services were discontinued in 1984. JEA were at Shoreham for five years before they closed in 1986. The Biggin Hill based company South-East Air then took over until their own collapse in 1988.

The fares charged for the Shoreham-Channel Islands services were very reasonable at the start: JFA only charged £15.30 return to Jersey in 1972, but by contrast the South-East fare to the Channel Islands was £80 return in 1986.

The last attempt to run a regular service was in 1991, when Marinair, in conjunction with Brymon Airways of Plymouth, opened a Saturdays-only service to Jersey for £99 return. They used 46-seat four engined D.H.Canada Dash 7's, but still could not make it pay.

## Air Races

"An integral part of running races at Shoreham is the sea fog which comes rolling in," wrote the "Royal Aero Club Gazette" in 1965. Nevertheless races have been held over the years as already mentioned in earlier chapters.

On August 28th 1954 a former wartime ferry pilot, Miss Freydis Leaf, won the Goodyear Trophy flying her Hawk Major G-ACYO at 139.5 m.p.h., and Fred Dunkerley was third with his Sparrowjet in the Southern Aero Club's race.

In 1962 the late Neil Williams, a famous aerobatic pilot, won Class I of the Shoreham races.

National Air Races were held at Shoreham in 1964 and 1965. In the latter year, Sheila Scott's Piper Comanche won a Ladies' Challenge Cup, with Mrs. Diana Barnato Walker (ex-ATA) coming in 3rd.

Sometimes Shoreham pilots won fame elsewhere. Charles Masefield, Beagle's demonstration pilot and son of Sir Peter, won the 1967 King's Cup race at Tollerton, Notts; his North American P-51D Mustang covered the course at 277.5 m.p.h. Seventeen years later, in 1984, Shoreham's catering manager, Kenneth Fehrenbach, won the King's Cup race at St. Athan in a Beagle Pup 100, in company with his daughter Mrs Susan Treague; The Queen presented him with the famous trophy.

In 1985 Shoreham was the venue for the King's Cup race for the first time since 1936. However, it was a bizarre race as 23 of the 26 contestants were disqualified for cutting corners or for flying too low. One did not finish, and of the two remaining competitors, Gordon Franks was declared the winner in a Siai-Marchetti SF. 260.

Sir Peter Masefield was the starter for the May 1991 Cecil Pashley centenary races to Abbeville and back, won by a Virgin Airways pilot, Timothy Bailey, in a Rutan Vari-Eze. His prize was the Brighton Aerial Cup, originally awarded in 1913.

The climax of Shoreham's racing history came in May 1994, when the revived Schneider Trophy race was held. No longer for seaplanes, as in 1913-1931, it attracted an entry of 35 light aircraft and the winner was Ian Finbow in a Piper PA-28 Cherokee. The event was repeated in July 1995 and was won by John Kelman at 189 m.p.h. in a Beechcraft Bonanza, G-COLA.

## Air Shows

Shoreham has always been known for its spectacular air shows since the Empire Air Days before WW II. This tradition has continued, and on May 30th 1959, the R.A.F.A.'s Brighton Air Week included the late Jeffrey Quill flying a Spitfire. It also brought to Shoreham one of the largest aircraft ever to land, the four-engined Blackburn Beverley transport.

In the early 1970s the Tiger Club held annual displays. The spectators witnessed aerobatics by well known pilots like Ray Hanna (Spitfire IX), the late Neil Williams (Pitts Special) and the 1960 World Aerobatic Champion, Ladislav Bezak of Czechoslovakia.

In 1977 Shoreham's air traffic control officers took over the running of the air displays, and in June an Avro Vulcan and the Battle of Britain Memorial Flight (Spitfire, Hurricane and Lancaster) gave unforgettable performances. So did Neil Williams in a 1943 Spitfire; tragically, only six months later both he and his wife died in the crash of a Casa Heinkel 111 in Spain.

The July 1980 show was a special one, marking the 70th anniversary of Harold Piffard's first flight from Shoreham on July 10th 1910. The venerable pioneer, the late Sir Thomas Sopwith, aged 92 (he lived to be over 100) sent a message: "I have many happy memories of my flying days at Shoreham so many years ago, and I send my best wishes to you and your staff at Shoreham on the occasion of your 70th anniversary".

September 1990 was another notable show, commemorating not only Shoreham's 80th birthday, but also 50 years since the Battle of Britain. Subsequent years have brought bigger and better programmes, culminating in 1995 with fly-pasts by Tucanos, Harriers, Lockheed Hercules, the re-built Blenheim IV, a Miles Magister, the amphibious Catalina (Canso), the Boeing B-17 Fortress "Sally B", and many more. The "Diamond Nine" Tiger Moths demonstrated formation flying, the Battle of Britain Memorial Flight revived wartime memories, and replicas of a Fokker Triplane and S.E.5As duelled in mock combat. On the ground the remains of a twin-boom Focke-Wulf 189, which crashed in Russia in 1943, were on display (prior to restoration).

## Notable Visitors

Shoreham's visitors over the years have included many distinguished people, both in aviation and in other walks of life. Royalty have graced the airfield with their presence from time to time in recent years. Prince Bernhard of the Netherlands opened the air show on May 30th 1959, and the

Duke of Edinburgh came on various dates in 1958, 1962 and 1968. On the last occasion he was flying a Beagle Pup.

Sir Harry Secombe, appearing in a show at Brighton, booked a weekend charter flight to Swansea and back in August 1959.

Oscar P. Jones, the famous Imperial Airways and BOAC captain, flew a Beagle Pup at Shoreham in October 1967; he had his first flight at Shoreham in 1917.

Squadron Leader Neville Duke, who set a world air speed record off the Sussex coast in 1953, test-flew the refurbished Miles-Dufon Student in January 1964.

Winston Churchil M.P., grandson of the wartime leader, refuelled his Piper Seneca at Shoreham in 1974. He was helping in the search for survivors from Sir Edward Heath's yacht, "Morning Cloud", which had sunk.

Group Captain Sir Douglas Bader DSO, DFC visited several times in his Miles Gemini.

Barry Sheene, the former world champion motor cyclist, qualified as a helicopter pilot with Spooner Aviation at Shoreham.

Ian Gow, the Eastbourne M.P. who was later murdered by the IRA, flew in the Trinity House service helicopter from Shoreham to the Royal Sovereign light vessel in August 1988.

Carol Barnes, the ITN newsreader, earned her wings in a Cessna 152 at Shoreham in September 1988.

The Duke of Kent arrived in a Wessex helicopter in 1989 to visit the Ricardo Engineering works.

## Some Interesting Visiting Aircraft

Early in April 1974, a North American B-25 Mitchell N76414C flew in for overhaul by Miles-Dufon. However it stayed for more than two years, because the pilot did not collect it! It was 30 years old, and had seen service in the Pacific in WW II; in 1968 it had been the "camera ship" during the making of the film "The Battle of Britain". Parking fees accumulated to well over £1000, and eventually in 1976 the airport authorities had to get High Court permission to sell it. The owner, an American named Jeff Hawke, then re-appeared, bought it back, and presented it to the Imperial War Museum collection at Duxford.

Other guests which outstayed their welcome were a Czech Morava 1200A twin left in 1985 for over a year, accruing £1775 in charges, and also a D.H. 104 Dove which was parked for several years up to 1990. The owner in Kent was sued from time to time, and eventually paid the charges due.

In March 1979 a Sikorsky Sea King helicopter of British Airways was used to test a sea anchor in the River Adur. In the same year two Canadian-built aircraft arrived at Shoreham: a D.H.C-5 Buffalo in June, and a D.H.C-4 Caribou of the Tanzanian Air Force in November.

In December 1984, a Junkers 52/3M was at Shoreham while doing some filming off Beachy Head.

In September 1990, Adrian Brook's restored Miles Magister was flown in by the then 79 year old George Miles!

Perhaps the most unusual aeroplane ever to come to Shoreham was a two-seat Mig-15-UT1 of the Polish Air Force. This renowned Russian-designed swept-wing jet fighter-trainer was bought by Graham Hinkley in 1992, and brought to Shoreham for restoration by Southern Air. It arrived by road, but by November 1993 it had been granted a CAA permit to test-fly. On November 19th 1993 it was flown out by Colonel Krzysztof Siek to Lydd and North Weald.

## International Arrivals

Over the years Shoreham has been the final destination for many aircraft from overseas, but among the more notable was the flight from Australia to England by Clive Canning in his home-built Thorpe 18 VH-CMC in 1976. As Federal President of the Ultra Light Aircraft Association in Australia, Clive's flight created great interest with the Popular Flying Association in the UK and he was afforded a great welcome at Shoreham on arrival. Clive Canning describes his epic journey in his book "Charlie Mike Charlie", and his graphic description of the last stage of his 16,000 km flight is reproduced here:

"Now the French shoreline was passing aft and the visibility was so unlimited I could see my goal on the horizon. Was it imagination? No, within a minute I confirmed it was very real, and with every second it came into better focus.

It was time to say goodbye to Paris and call London Control. Can you imagine the feeling? "London Control, this is Victor Hotel, Charlie Mike Charlie, at Echo Bravo, time 1134 (GMT), cruising 6000 ft. estimating Shoreham at 1149 (GMT), will take descent when convenient".

"Victor Mike Charlie, welcome sir, we have been wondering about your arrival, no known traffic for your descent, please call Shoreham Tower 125.4 ten miles south". It is natural in moments like this, to think that something will surely foul up that last few miles. My eyes scanned the instrument gauges but then I relaxed, and just burst into song. The big chimney stacks of the Brighton and Hove power station came into view like gigantic sign posts pointing the way. Now I was calling "Shoreham Tower, Victor Hotel, Charlie Mike Charlie is 10 miles south of Shoreham inbound 2000 ft., landing instructions please". "Victor Mike Charlie, Shoreham Tower reading you loud and clear, please let us be the first to congratulate you and request you join right base for a run along 07 at 500 ft. so that we may time you officially across the line; please report turning final".

As Clive taxied into the Customs parking bay he was humbled to see the Australian Flag flying from the Control Tower in his honour and the controllers leaning out of the windows. The welcoming committee of the Popular Flying Association were waiting to greet him and to share his glorious moment.

Clive Canning had left Moorabbin Airport in Melbourne on June 12th 1976 and arrived at Shoreham on July 1st, just one day later than planned. A remarkable achievement in a journey which was full of hazards, which included his own private dog-fight with a pair of Mig 21s over Syria.

The Miles M. 77 Sparrowjet at Shoreham in 1954. Note the beacon on top of the control tower.
Photo: Peter G. Campbell.

The Meteor FR.9 VZ 608 modified by F.G. Miles Ltd. in 1955-56 as a test-bed for Rolls Royce.
Photo: Peter G. Campbell.

George Miles about to test fly the Bristol Boxkite replica built in 1964 for the film "Those Magnificent Men And Their Flying Machines".
Photo: Miles Aircraft Ltd./Adwest Archives.

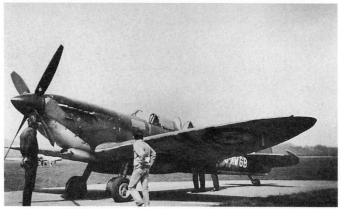

Former well-known fighters in civilian guise at Shoreham. Top, Hawker
Hurricane G-AWLW and, above, a two-seat Spitfire G-AWGB.
Photos: Rex Ingram.

An RAF Vickers Varsity at Shoreham in the late 1950s prepares to take-off.
Photo: The Shoreham Airport Collection.

Grahame Gates taken in 1990.

The Miles M.115 prototype (later to become the Beagle-Miles M.218) seen here in the snow
at Shoreham in the winter of 1962.
Photo: Grahame Gates.

The M.115 being flown by George Miles over the South Downs north of Portslade.
Photo: Grahame Gates.

The first production model of the B.206-Z1 (the military version) which was later named the Basset, seen here off Beachy Head.
Photo: Grahame Gates.

The first protype Beagle Pup G-AVDF in 1967.
Photo: Grahame Gates.

The new-look Air Traffic Control Tower added in 1986. Note the replica Avro 504K in the foreground, present for a R.A.F.A. Air Display.
Photo: The Shoreham Airport Collection.

A Twin-Otter of Jersey European Airways and a Britten-Norman Islander of Haywards
Aviation on the apron at Shoreham around 1980.
Photo: The Shoreham Airport Collection.

The high-tech jet age comes to Shoreham. A "Jumpjet" Harrier GR.7 of No. 20 Reserve
Squadron seen here during the R.A.F.A. Display in September 1994.
Photo: The Shoreham Airport Collection.

# Chapter 11 THE HARD RUNWAY CONTROVERSY 1969–1981

All through its long history, Shoreham's low-lying airfield has suffered badly from flooding. The River Adur flows along its eastern perimeter, and heavy rains invariably produced a water-logged field. In 1977-78 the Airport had to close for 39 days between October and February.

As long ago as 1964, the technical manager of South Coast Air Taxis was calling for a 1,500-yard (1,372-metre) east-west runway suitable for Bristol Freighters and Short Skyvans. Pressure built up over the years, for and against; many local people were opposed because of aircraft noise - among them the local MP, Captain Henry Kerby.

## Public Inquiries

In April 1969, the then Ministry of Housing and Local Government held a public inquiry at the Lancing Parish Hall at which Quintin Hogg (now Lord Hailsham) put the case for the runway. A retired surgeon put a counter view, and showed slides which portrayed the bad effects of noise on cats' kidneys and human organs . . .

The Beagle collapse did not help the Airport's case, and the inquiry was re-opened in 1970. The Minister, Anthony Greenwood, accepted his inspector's view and turned down the proposal for an east-west runway (which would have meant aircraft movements over residential areas in both directions). However, he said that a NE/SW runway was "not at issue". The Municipal Airport Joint Committee took the hint and put in a new application for a runway in that direction.

Lancing Parish Hall was again packed out in February 1972 when the inquiry next opened; Shoreham's new MP, Richard Luce, was among those who opposed. The West Sussex County Planning Officer told the inquiry he would welcome the closure of the Airport. The Secretary of State for the Environment, Peter Walker, did not go so far as that, but he refused the application because, he said, the Airport was too closely confined by houses, the railway line, and main roads.

The first sign of a breakthrough came in October 1976, when the West Sussex County Planning Committee approved the idea of a hard runway. The proposal moved on at a snail's pace, but the Department of Transport again refused the proposal two years later.

However when the third public inquiry was held in March 1980, opponents had a shock when the Department of Transport reversed its view and said it now supported the runway. Later that year the Junior Trade Minister, Norman Tebbit, announced Government aid to improve 12 regional airports, including an allocation of £250,000 for Shoreham's runway.

## Formal Government Approval

Government approval was finally given by Michael Heseltine in June 1981, but he attached strict conditions: the runway length was to be limited to 760 metres (830 yards), it was to be used only between 7 a.m. and 9 p.m., and there were to be not more than 75,000 movements a year. The approval was timely as Shoreham had just had another spell of bad weather which closed the airfield for 49 days in three months.

S.M. Tidy (Public Works) Ltd. of Brighton beat eight other firms for the contract, and work began on October 12th 1981. Eight thousand tons of stabilised, pulverised fuel ash from Brighton B power station provided the foundation, with hot-rolled asphalt on top. Scheduled to be completed in four months, the work was delayed by rain, snow, flooding and problems with materials. It was not until September 18th 1982 that it was officially opened.

To mark the occasion, a 150 ft. Skyship 500 visited Shoreham, rather inappropriately, as an airship is one type of aircraft that needs no runway!

## Continuing Controversy

The controversy over the future of the airfield was not laid to rest even after the runway was finally constructed, and in 1986 the Joint Committee went so far as to call for tenders for the

Airport, and seven serious offers were forthcoming. However, at the last moment the Committee drew back. The local press, however, continued to stir and over the years have advocated its privatisation. Suggestions have been made for its sale as a golf course or housing estates. As recently as February 24th 1988, the Editorial in the Brighton "Evening Argus" raised the topic once more and said "the site would be worth millions for housing and could solve a lot of the area's problems". (See Appendix for a selection of letters to the Editor of the "Evening Argus.")

## New Air Traffic Control Tower, 1986

With the new runway in operation, more than a dozen years after the first public inquiry, Shoreham could have more confidence in its future. Then another problem arose. While Stavers H. Tiltman's handsome Art Deco design for the 1936 Terminal Building was admired, and English Heritage had ranked it as a Grade II Listed Building, it had disadvantages for air traffic control purposes. A critical CAA report in 1986 convinced the Municipal Joint Committee that a new tower had to be built at a cost of £45,000. Planning approval was granted and English Heritage agreed to the design which enlarged the control tower without impairing the general appearance of the building. Work began in late November 1987.

For the next three months the air traffic officers operated from a temporary portable building. Gales delayed construction, but by March 1988 the new tower was in service. At 70 ft. above the ground, Peter Dickerson (SATCO) and his team of three colleagues, Mary Snelling, John Haffenden and Richard Almond, had a greatly enhanced view in all directions with sloping anti-reflective glass windows in keeping with modern design.

# Chapter 12   A MISCELLANY

## *No. 277 Squadron Re-unions*

The valiant deeds of Shoreham's wartime Air Sea Rescue Squadron have been recorded in Chapter 5. However, the first reunion was not held until September 5th 1987, and this was entirely due to enthusiastic research by Richard Almond of the air traffic control staff. He got in touch with past Squadron members, and as a result 30 of them came for the day. Nick Grace flew his Spitfire IX which reminded them of their own Spitfire days, and then John Turner demonstrated his "Forwarder" (a modified version of the wartime Fairchild Argus with an in-line engine). Flt. Lt. Keith "Kiwi" Saunders (retd.) DFC, RNZAF, then unveiled a plaque to 277 Squadron in the Terminal Building. Among those present was Dr. (formerly Flt. Lt.) Ken Creamer, the Shoreham Flight Commander.

Local resident Les "Dizzy" Seales, a 277 Squadron air-gunner who lives at Shoreham beach, organised the next reunion at the Airport on September 22nd 1990. An ASR Squadrons Association was formed, linking the four units (Nos. 275, 276, 277 and 278) which had provided wartime coverage round the coasts from Scotland to Cornwall, and their first gathering was at Harrowbeer, Plymouth, in 1990. Shoreham was the next venue on June 8th 1991, when 53 members and wives attended. Next year everyone went to Aylsham in Norfolk, but came back to Shoreham again on September 11th 1993. Further Squadron dinners were held on July 30th 1994 and August 12th 1995.

## *TV and Films*

Shoreham's 1936 Terminal Building still retains much of the atmosphere of that age, and consequently it has been popular with TV and film directors.

In the 1960s the TV "Troubleshooters" programme filmed the actor Robert Hardy as Sir Winston Churchill in the passenger hall at the airport.

In November 1962, a sequence for the film "The Running Man" was shot at Shoreham, in which a Kranich sailplane (SE-SCC) was purposely ditched in the sea off Shoreham on November 15th.

In May 1968 the Vickers Gunbus replica G-ATVP (painted as 2345) was at Shoreham filming for "Oh What a Lovely War" starring Richard Attenborough.

In September 1971 BBC cameras were present filming a programme which included a Fairey Swordfish, a replica Fokker E3 Eindekker, a Caudron G3 and a Morane-Saulnier 203.

In June 1984 Shoreham became "Changi Airport" in Singapore for three days. The BBC "Tenko" series featured women in a Japanese prisoner-of-war camp, and their final release in 1945. A Dakota provided the flying shots and once again the airport passenger hall was used. The cameraman narrowly missed a shot of Lancing College Chapel in the background! The stars were Emily Bolton and Burt Kwouk.

In November 1986 another BBC series dramatised Olivia Manning's "Balkan Trilogy" novels under the title "The Fortunes of War". A Junkers 52/3M landed at Shoreham for a sequence involving Kenneth Branagh, Emma Thompson and Alan Bennett.

In 1990 Dame Agatha Christie's Hercule Poirot novels took on a new lease of life on television, thanks to the inspired acting of David Suchet as the Belgian detective, and commercial TV filmed "Death in the Clouds", with sequences at Shoreham Airport.

In 1995 Sir Ian McKellen's version of Shakespeare's "Richard III" used Shoreham for a sequence. Unbelievably, aircraft come into this version, and  involved a Dakota G-AMRA from Air Atlantique, painted in Pan American Airways colours, and a D.H. 89A Rapide G-AEML.

The BBC comedy show "Waiting for God" also used Shoreham in one of the episodes.

No. 277 Squadron's Badge (Crown Copyright Right Reserved) is reproduced here by the courtesy of Group Captain Ian Madelin, head of the Air Historical Branch at the Ministry of Defence.

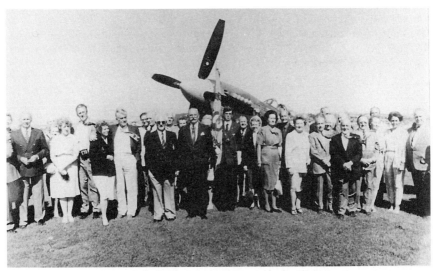

Some faces to go with the names; No. 277 Squadron reunion at Shoreham September 10th 1987. Just out of the picture, extreme left Sqn. Ldr. Len Healey DFC, DFM. Then left to right: Mrs Joan Goater (only half face) who worked in the YMCA canteen 1942-44 (sister of D.L. Bird). Fifth from left (camera at waist) Dennis L. Bird. Seventh from left, Flt. Lt. "Kiwi" Saunders DFC, RNZAF. Eighth from left (back row in white jacket) Flt. Lt. (now Dr.) Ken Creamer, Shoreham Flight Commander. Tenth from left (in dark glasses) Flt. Lt. Tom Fletcher, DFC, DFM and bar. Under Spitfire cockpit (bald head) Flt. Lt. Johnny Barber DFM. Two to the right from Barber, (tie askew) Les Orrock, ground staff. Fifth from right (striped tie) Fg. Off. Les "Dizzy" Seales.

## The Discovery of the Unexploded German bomb (1982)

While Shoreham survived many bombing raids in the war, those troubled days left an unexpected legacy. In November 1981, a bomb disposal unit (No. 49 EOD Squadron, Royal Engineers, Chatham) was called in as it was thought that TIPE mines (pipes filled with high explosives designed to explode when trodden on) might still be buried under the surface, and could be a hazard for workers involved on the new hard runway. Major Guy Lucas and his men did in fact find some, but they also found something else. On February 11th 1982 they found the German unexploded bomb mentioned in Chapter 5. It was 5 ft. long, 500 lb. No. 158 D 40 and marked with a Nazi Eagle. It appears that attempts had been made to recover it in 1941, but the hole kept filling up with water and in the end they just left it. 41 years later it took the Royal Engineers seven hours to defuse it, and they finally gave the all-clear at 1.30 a.m. on March 31st 1982. The bomb casing was handed over to Councillor Derek Ireland, Chairman of the Municipal Joint Committee for display in the Airport Terminal.

## Airport Tenants, Past and Present

**Southern Aero Club**  Originally founded in 1913 by Cecil Pashley as the Sussex County Aero Club, it was among the first flying clubs in the country. After WW I it was re-named the Southern Aero Club in 1926 until the advent of the South Coast Flying Club in 1935. It reverted to its former name again in 1952 as recorded in earlier chapters. With its club-room and bar, it was a popular social centre run by the Pashleys until his death in 1969. Colin and Linda Cleaver took over the club in February 1989. It finally closed in 1992, 79 years after its foundation.

## Present tenants (based on listing in "Pilot" magazine, April 1996)

**Air Base Flying Club**  (Newly formed, not yet listed, 120 members.

**Air South**  Airline pilot John Pothecary first flew into Shoreham in 1951 as a visitor; later his Comper Swift became a regular sight. He helped form the Southern Strut branch of the Popular Flying Association, and in 1972 he and his wife Jenny set up Air South in the former drawing office of F.G. Miles Ltd. John began as CFI, but his flying duties with Air UK meant that Jenny, a former BUA air hostess and qualified instructor, took over the running of the club. She was CFI from 1979 to 1985. The Air South Flying Group* has the largest fleet of aircraft at Shoreham, with six modern types and two veterans - a 1933 Tiger Moth and a 1945 Piper Cub. Air South also has an Engineering section, working on both vintage and current types.

(*As we went to press we learnt that the Air South Flying Group had been taken over by Southern Air Ltd.)

**Barry Aviation**  50 members, two aircraft.

**Fast Helicopters Ltd**.  Also based at Thruxton. Two helicopters at Shoreham.

**Premier Flying and Social Club**  250 members, two aircraft.

**Sky Leisure Aviation Ltd.**  300 members, seven aircraft.

**Southern Air Ltd.**  This company has fixed-wing aircraft and helicopters for charter and flying training. In 1982 they became the sole distributors in the British Isles for Hughes Helicopters International (now McDonnell Douglas). Southern Air also assemble Enstrom helicopters.

**Sussex Flying Club** This was the Southern Aero Club's immediate successor and was formed in 1992 by two of the former Clubs' instructors, James Crabbe and Michael Stott. Its fleet includes various Cessnas and a twin-engined Piper Aztec.

**Warbird Flying Club** 25 members, one aircraft, (ex US Navy 1941 North American Harvard T-6 owned by Andrew Edie).

**Chelsea/Northbrook College** The Chelsea College of Aeronautical Engineering was founded in London in 1924, and an early pupil was Amy Johnson. As recorded earlier in Chapter 7, the College was at Redhill aerodrome before moving to Shoreham in July 1975. Among the College's patrons was Group Captain Sir Douglas Bader DSO, DFC and a year after he died in 1982, Lady Bader opened the Bader Centre at the College containing nine lecture rooms and a library. Chelsea College courses were particularly popular with overseas countries, but the world recession in the mid-1980s led to a dramatic drop in student numbers. By July 1986 it looked as if the Chelsea College would have to close, but West Sussex County Council came to the rescue. A merger with two other Sussex colleges led to the formation of the "Northbrook College of Design and Technology" with purpose-built headquarters at Northbrook Farm, which is at Durrington, near Worthing.

In July 1987 16 year-old Amanda Oakley became the first girl trainee engineer at the College in 63 years. A year later another student, Thomas Durnford, won a £250 prize for designing the new Shoreham Airport emblem which adorns all the publicity material. It is a stylised representation of the Terminal Building with its new control tower:

**Popular Flying Association (PFA)** The PFA celebrates its golden anniversary in 1996, and it has based its national headquarters at Shoreham Airport for nearly a quarter of a century. Founded in 1946 as the Ultra-Light Aircraft Association, its purposes are to promote facilities for light aviation in the UK, to bring together air-minded people of all kinds, and in particular to help those who wish to own an aircraft themselves, or even to build one from plans or kits. The PFA is recognised by the Sports Council and the Civil Aviation Authority, and PFA inspectors supervise members' maintenance and servicing of their aircraft, under the "Permit to Fly" scheme. The 8,500 members are organised in local branches called "Struts". Anthony Preston is the PFA's General Manager, and they produce the bi-monthly magazine "Popular Flying."

**D-Day Museum** Some years ago Ken Rimell of Bosham opened an Aviation Museum at Apuldram, near Chichester, which had been an advanced landing ground used for D-Day in 1944. Just in time for the 50th anniversary of that historic event, the collection moved to Shoreham Airport; it was opened as the Museum of D-Day Aviation on April 2nd 1994 by Flt. Lt. Tom Fletcher, whose brave air-sea rescue exploits from Shoreham earned him a DFC, DFM and bar. The Museum is a fascinating commemoration of wartime days. It has a complete RAF ASR launch, a replica Spitfire, part of the fuselage of an Airspeed Horsa troop-carrying glider and many other artefacts. Special displays feature Air Chief Marshal Sir Harry Broadhurst, and the story of ASR both airborne and seaborne. One of the volunteer helpers at the Museum is the former Flying Officer Leslie "Dizzy" Seales of 277 Squadron.

**Other Users** Many firms and organisations have based themselves at Shoreham since the war. Some are no longer there like SCAT (South Coast Air Taxis), Toon Ghose Aviation, Frank Hewitt's Shoreham School of Flying, Spooner Aviation, Rollason's Flying Group, British Caledonian Helicopters, Meridian Airmaps Ltd., Miles-Dufon, and the Aerodyne aircraft components factory.

Others still flourish, such as the eight flying clubs and other training organisations already listed. Also aircraft maintenance and repair companies such as C.J. Fox, Jade Air Engineering Ltd., and KB Aviation.

From 1988 the Sussex County Police helicopter unit has been located at Shoreham, and was the subject of a half-hour TV programme in February 1996.

Many people look to Shoreham Airport for tuition, air charter, servicing, employment, air shows, and leisure. Social activities thrive; the southern branch of the Spitfire Society meets monthly for talks by notable speakers such as Gp. Capt. Hamish Mahaddie, Lettice Curtis (former ATA pilot) and the CO of the Battle of Britain Memorial Flight. The Terminal Building has a comfortable bar and restaurant which serves breakfasts, lunches and teas.

David Dunstall and Mike Williams administer The Shoreham Airport Collection on a voluntary basis. They offer an archive and research facility and provide regular airport tours.

## Ricardo Consulting Engineers

While not a tenant of the airfield, Ricardo's works situated on the northern boundary had close links with the airfield during the war as will be recalled from Chapter 5. In the "Shoreham Herald" of February 23rd 1996 it was reported that Ricardo's had won a contract to overhaul Spitfire Rolls Royce Merlin engines (a role it undertook in the war years). The many restorations being undertaken on Spitfires around the world has created a demand that Ricardo's were well placed to meet. So once again history in and around the Airport has repeated itself.

## Accidents

Flying nowadays is quite a safe activity compared with other forms of transport. Shoreham did have somewhat hazardous conditions in its early days with open ditches on its boundaries and HT power lines close to its northern perimeter. Natural obstacles can be removed, but there is always the risk of pilot error or mechanical failure at a critical moment, and as already recorded, there have been crashes at Shoreham over the years.

One opponent of the hard runway sought to support her case by pointing to 11 notifiable accidents in 7 years. Considering that there were 40,000 movements a year at the time, which included the test flying of new aircraft by Beagle Aircraft, that is not a bad record.

In the last 32 years there have been 14 fatal accidents, either at the Airport or within the district. Most were due to mechanical problems, and occasionally pilot error, but none have involved the injury of local citizens. Indeed pilot skill in avoiding houses was a feature of the accident which occurred on March 2nd 1996, when a Jodel D.9 suffered power loss on the approach, and narrowly missed houses in Lancing before crashing into a field. Sadly the pilot, Malcolm Allen, lost his life. Details of these accidents are listed in the Appendix.

## Shoreham Personalities

Over the post-war years, a number of personalities have left their mark on the story of Shoreham Airport. Here are just a few of them:

## Cecil Laurence Pashley MBE, AFC (1891-1969)

The most famous of all the characters at Shoreham, "Pash's" whole life revolved around flying, with the wholehearted support of his wife Vera. In a working career of nearly 60 years, he logged over 20,000 flying hours. It was an unwelcome shock when, in December 1965, the Ministry of

Aviation refused to renew his pilot's licence. Then aged 74, he fought to have his case reviewed. The Ministry relented, restoring his licence, provided he always flew accompanied by another licensed pilot.

One of his pupils, Lionel Hill of Bognor, gave a very personal impression of him in the February 1988 issue of "Flypast" (while air testing an Avro 504K). "Pashley was quietly spoken and of very small stature, with small hands and feet. I could only just see the top of Pashley's bare head (he never wore a helmet). Suddenly, almost roughly, he pulled the Avro into a vertical climb and at the top cut the engine causing the Avro to shudder for a moment and then fall away in a steep dive in the opposite direction - the famous Immelmann turn. It certainly took my breath away. I was also taught by the other instructor, F.G. Miles, and immediately noticed that his touch on the controls was much rougher than Pashley's".

Cecil Pashley died on December 10th 1969 aged 77, having been awarded the MBE in 1948 and the Livery of the Guild of Air Pilots and Air Navigators (GAPAN) in 1964. When the centenary of his birth came round on May 14th 1991, Shoreham put on a "Pashley weekend" two days earlier. A solitary Tiger Moth that he had used flew over his grave in Mill Lane Cemetery in Shoreham. Royal Aero Club races to Abbeville and back were held in his honour, and the Moth Diamond Nine team looped over the airfield. Sir Peter Masefield opened an exhibition at Shoreham-by-Sea's Marlipins Museum, and later at the Airport he unveiled a plaque to Pashley in the Terminal Building. A portait of "Pash" painted by his daughter Nonie was presented to the Southern Aero Club, and the eastern perimeter road was formally named "Pashley Way" in his honour. So his friends and colleagues commemorated a great aviator. His wife Vera, who was always so totally supportive of him in all his activities, lives on in her nineties.

She enjoyed the social evenings at the Southern Aero Club, and before that the South Coast Flying Club, and when "Pash" was honoured for reaching 10,000 hours in 1939, she made the comment "When I am a quiet old lady, the memories of the happy hours we have shared with our friends, will at least enable us to remain young at heart".

### Alexander Ewen Gunn MBE (b.1924)

Another remarkable figure at Shoreham was Benn Gunn, a doughty Scot who was the Airport Manager from 1971 until his retirement in March 1990. A Cranwell pupil in 1942, he flew Spitfires in No. 501 Squadron and Tempests in No. 274, and shot down the last V-1 flying bomb over England. After the war he was Chief Test Pilot for Boulton Paul Aircraft of Wolverhampton for 17 years before joining Beagle at Shoreham in 1967 as a marketing manager.

As Airport Manager he was forceful and effective, and in May 1988 he tackled head-on those critics who complained at the annual deficits which the Municipal Joint Committee had to make good. "Why should a Municipal Airport make a profit?" he demanded. "Does a park or a school?"

He thought the Airport should be regarded as an amenity, or as a civic necessity "like the Mayor's car". During his time Shoreham won the coveted AOPA Sword in 1988, awarded by the Aircraft Owners' and Pilots' Association for the Best Airport of the Year. This was in competition with the big league - the previous winner was Elmdon (Birmingham). To crown his career, Ben was awarded the MBE in the New Year Honours list of 1990.

### John Haffenden

Ben Gunn was succeeded first by John Larkin, and then there was a duopoly consisting of Charles Hall as Facilities Manager and John Haffenden as Operations Manager. Finally, from April 1995, John was officially put in charge of all operations as General Manager. John has spent all his working life at Shoreham Airport, recounting with pleasure how he was the last employee engaged by Cecil Pashley to work ("as a Boy Friday") at the Southern Aero Club in 1968. He later helped out in the air traffic control tower, and took his ATC licence in 1973. In 1990 he became Senior

Controller. Now, as General Manager, he will take Shoreham Airport forward into the second half of the 1990s.

## Frederick George Miles (1903-1976)

The Miles brothers have an assured place in the history of British aviation. Their return to Shoreham in 1951 and their involvement in Beagle have already been recounted. "FG" lived on until August 15th 1976, dying in a Worthing nursing home at the age of 73. His wife Maxine (the famous "Blossom", daughter of the actor Sir Johnston Forbes-Robertson) survived until 1984. His younger brother George H. Miles (b.1912) is still alive, but has moved away from his native Sussex to Edinburgh.

## Toon Ghose

Another colourful figure in Shoreham's history is Toon Ghose, who left Calcutta in 1955 on a Vespa motor-scooter; having reached France, he learnt to glide and set up an Indian world glider record of 25,000 ft. He then learned to fly powered aircraft, married an English wife, and took his commercial pilot's licence in England. By 1968 he was CFI at Cecil Pashley's Southern Aero Club. In the 1970s he set up Toon Ghose Aviation at Shoreham, but sadly it went into voluntary liquidation in April 1983.

## Richard M. Almond (1942-1991)

For more than 25 years Richard Almond devoted much of his leisure time to researching the history of Shoreham Airport. This is the book he would like to have written, had not an untimely death robbed him of the opportunity. Richard was in the RAF for five years, serving in the Middle and Far East. In 1964 he joined the ATC staff at Shoreham. He had suggested that the Gunnery Trainer Dome at the north-west corner of the airfield should become the Airport Museum, but it was burned out in 1969 by arsonists. In 1977 his prompt warning saved the lives of three boys he spotted playing on the railway in the path of a train. Ten years later he organised the first reunion of 277 Squadron, as described earlier. Sadly, by 1990 he was seriously ill with cancer, but he came to the September reunion. He died on February 22nd 1991, but he will be long remembered. His 17 scrapbooks, each an inch thick and measuring 8" x 12", must run to over 1000 pages . . . in themselves a worthy epitaph.

## Conclusion

This concludes Part 4 which shows how financial deficits, economic recessions, unexploded bombs, public inquiries and press attacks have all done their utmost to destroy Shoreham Airport in the last 43 years, but it has survived thanks to the dogged determination of its staff and users. Even as we go to press there are reports of moves to privatise the airport and remove it from Municipal control. Whatever its future, it is hoped that Shoreham Airport will continue to serve the community and build its history on into the 21st century.

# BIBLIOGRAPHY

ASWORTH, Chris, "Action Stations 9", Military Airfields of Central South and South East England, Patrick Stephens Ltd., 1985.

BAGLEY, John A., "Shoreham and Ford: The History of Two Sussex Airfields".

BRETT, R. Dallas, OBE, "Schoolboy Memoirs", "Aeroplane Monthly," Dec. 1979.

BROOKS, Robin, J., "Sussex Airfields in the Second World War", Countryside Books , 1993.

BROOKS, Roy, "Sussex Flights and Fliers 1783-1919", Downside Publications, 1992.

BROWN, Don L, "Wings Over Sussex", "Aeroplane Monthly", Sept, Oct. 1979.

BROWN, Don L, "Miles Aircraft Since 1925", Putnam, 1970.

CAMPBELL, Peter G., "The Fifties Revisited: An Aerobiography", Cirrus Associates, 1994.

"Shoreham Airport : A Record of Visiting Aircraft 1946-1970", Cirrus Associates, 1996.

CRUDDAS, Colin, "In Cobhams' Company", Cobham plc, 1994.

FORREST, Sqn. Ldr., J. A., "Close Encounters of a V-1 Kind" or "Grandfather's Flying Bomb", 1994.

FRANKS, Norman, "Another Kind of Courage", Patrick Stephens Ltd., 1994.

HARWOOD, Ian, "Gull Genesis", "Aeroplane Monthly", June 1994.

JACKSON, Aubrey J., "British Civil Aircraft 1919-1972", Vols. 1 & 2, Putnam, 1973 and 1974.

JOHNSTON, Johnnie and Laddie Lucas, "Glorious Summer", Stanley Paul.

LEWIS, Peter, "British Aircraft 1809-1914", Putnam.

McINTOSH, W/C R. H., DFC, AFC , "All Weather Mac", Macdonald.

TEMPLE, Julian, "Wings Over Woodley", Aston Publications Ltd.1987.

THORNHILL, J. M., "The History of Architecture and Design 1890-1978: Shoreham Airport", 1981.


"The Illustrated Encyclopedia of Aircraft" Orbis Publishing Ltd.


**Periodicals**
"Aero"
"Aeroplane Monthly"
"The Aeroplane"
"Flypast"
"Flight"
The Lancing College Magazine
The Lancing Club Newsletter
"The Miles Magazine"
"The Shoreham Airport Society Magazine"

**Newspapers**
"Adur Herald"
"Brighton and Hove Gazette"
"Evening Argus"
"Sussex Daily News"
"Shoreham Herald"
"Worthing Herald"

**Unpublished Articles**
The Richard Almond Collection scrapbooks.
Grahame Gates, AFRAeS diary extracts 1951-1964; and "British Flight Manuals" July 1959 to April 1964.
Gary Sunderland, C.P. Eng., M.I.E. Aust.: transcript of tape recording made by Charles Gates in 1984.
Tape recording of Charles Gates recalling his life at Shoreham by courtesy of Grahame Gates.
The late Sqn. Ldr. L.R. Healey, DFC, DFM. 1944 War Diary.

**Articles**
Richard M. Almond. Articles in air show programmes 1979 & 1980.
Lionel Hill. Article in "Early Days", "Flypast" Feb. 1988.
Michael Jerram. "The Beagle Fiasco" in "Pilot", April, May, June, and July 1983.
Gordon Roberts. "Shoreham Airport Leading the Way", in "Wingspan" April 1990.
Robert Thompson. Article on MIG-15-UTL in "Air Display International" June/July 1994.

# APPENDIX PART 1

Report from Captain W.D. Beatty on the suitability of Shoreham as a Squadron station.
To Officer Commanding, Royal Flying Corps.
I visited the Shoreham Aerodrome on Saturday 28th April (1913), and in company with Mr. Gonne, Secretary of the company owning the aerodrome, inspected the landing ground and sheds.
AREA: The landing ground consists of an area of about 150 acres of flat grass land, bounded on the north and east by a corrugated iron fence, on the south by a railway embankment and on the west by the cart track from "Honeyman's Hole" to "New Salts Farm". The boundaries are marked in red on the attached map. This area is at present grazed by the occupiers of "Lee's Barn".

The company owning the aerodrome has also, I understand, options over land marked in green, lying to the west and south, amounting to about another 150 acres.

The existing landing ground would, however, appear to be of ample size for a squadron station.
SURFACE: The fences marked on the map have been removed and the ditches filled in, with the exception of a few on the northern portion of the ground, marked in blue.
SHEDS: The existing sheds are situated at the south-east corner of the ground and consist of one block of seven sheds each 45 ft. by 45 ft., and one 50 ft. They are built of corrugated iron and wood with earth floors. They are not of sufficiently sound construction to be worth expenditure on alterations or upkeep. In addition to the sheds there is a small office, and two small bungalows of wood construction which are used as club rooms.

All the buildings are dangerously situated as regards fire risk being at the foot of the railway embankment. I believe one fire has already occurred here.
SQUADRON SHEDS: If sheds were to be built here for a squadron they should be sited along the northern boundary, which would also be the most convenient site as regards delivery of materials and stores.
BARRACKS: If barracks are to be built for a squadron here it will probably be inadvisable on hygienic grounds to site them on the low-lying land of the aerodrome. Rising ground to the north-west, or across the river above Old Shoreham, offer possible sites, but as regards the latter site see under ACCESS below.
WATER: The springs feeding "Honeyman's Hole" are said to give a good supply of very pure water (see historical note on the origins of the name, next page).
ACCESS: Shoreham Station is about 1½ miles from the landing ground, but the road passes over "Old Shoreham Bridge". This is an old pile bridge with a low limit of weight for vehicles passing over it and there are also certain tolls payable e.g. 6d for a motor car.

It would appear therefore that Worthing would be the rail depot from which to draw stores. Worthing station is however about five miles from the ground and the road is not good and would probably cut up a good deal under heavy lorries.
SURROUNDING COUNTRY: The surrounding country appears very good for flying over being open downland. Owing to the comparative absence of trees and hedges, it should be possible to land in safety almost anywhere for several miles around; though, of course, as elsewhere in England a considerable proportion of the land is covered with growing crops in the summer and early autumn.
FOGS : Shoreham District in common with the rest of the South Coast suffers somewhat from sea fog. But so far as I can ascertain fog is not more prevalent there than in say the Farnborough-Reading district.
(Signed) W.D. Beatty Capt. 1/5/13

CAPT. BEATTY'S MAP OF
SHOREHAM AERODROME
1913

<u>LEGEND</u>

– – – Boundary of land
owned by Brighton
and Shoreham
Aerodrome 1913

Open ditches not filled
in at northern end.

xxxxxxxxxxx
Boundaries of land to the
west and south over which
options were also held.

## HISTORICAL NOTE ON THE ORIGINS OF THE NAME "HONEYMAN'S HOLE"

(12ft to 15ft diameter and 6ft to 8ft deep. Water bubbles up to the surface through a fragmented chalk bottom.)

In a letter dated 1979, Charles Gates revealed some interesting folk-lore which had it that a horse and dray complete with driver had fallen into the hole and were never seen again! Presumably Honeyman was the driver, and this name has survived to the present day, rather than the alternative "Dead Man's Hole", used when the Old Sussex Pad was a haunt of smugglers. (The Old Sussex Pad was burnt down in 1905.)

# APPENDIX PART 2

Record of F.G. Miles' early flying from Shoreham (by courtesy of Peter Amos, The Miles Aircraft Collection).

Frederick George Miles, 42 St Aubyns, Hove, Sussex.

Date of birth: 22nd March 1903.

No. of licence:ß  Aero Club 9003

AB 910 ( B licence)

| DATE | AIRCRAFT | | JOURNEY | TIME IN AIR | REMARKS | |
|---|---|---|---|---|---|---|
| **1925** | **Type** | **Reg.No.** | | **Min.** | | |
| Nov 26th | Avro | G-EATU | Aerodrome | .30 | Tuition (C.P.) | |
| Nov 29th | " | " | " | .18 | " | " |
| Dec 1st | " | " | " | .15 | " | " |
| Dec 2nd | " | " | " | .15 | " | " |
| Dec 3rd | " | " | " | .30 | " | " |
| Dec 5th | " | " | " | .10 | " | " |
| Dec 6th | " | " | " | .15 | " | " |
| Dec 11th | " | " | " | .15 | " | " |
| Page total carried fwd. | | | | 2.28 | " | " |
| Dec 12th | " | " | " | .15 | " | " |
| Dec 13th | " | " | " | .30 | " | " |
| Dec 16th | " | " | " | .25 | " | " |
| Dec 17th | " | " | " | .15 | " | " |
| **1926** | | | | | | |
| Jan 8th | " | " | " | .20 | " | " |
| Jan 16th | " | " | " | .20 | " | " |
| Feb 4th | " | " | " | .20 | " | " |
| Feb 4th | " | " | " | .25 | " | " |
| Page total brought fwd. | | | | 5.18 | Tuition (C.P.) | |
| Feb 4th | " | | Torr Hill | .30 | " | " |
| Feb 11th | | | Aerodrome | .20 | " | " |
| Feb 11th | " | " | " | .25 | " | " |
| Feb 21st | " | " | " | .25 | " | " |
| Feb 28th | " | " | " | .20 | " | " |
| Feb 28th | " | " | " | .15 | " | " |
| Mar 14th | " | " | " | .21 | " | " |
| Mar 14th | " | " | " | .20 | " | " |
| Page total brought fwd. | | | | 8.14 | Tuition (C.P.) | |
| Mar 14th | " | " | " | .20 | " | " |
| Mar 26th | " | " | " | .40 | Landings | " | " |
| Mar 28th | " | " | " | .40 | " | " |
| Mar 30th | " | " | " | .10 | " | " |
| Apr 1st | " | " | " | 25 | " | " |
| Apr 3rd | " | " | " | .0 | " | " |
| Apr 23rd | " | " | " | .25 | " | " |
| Apr 23rd | " | " | " | .25 | " | " |
| Page total brought fwd | | | | 11.29 | Tuition (C.P.) | |
| May 1st | " | " | " | .15 | " | " |

(continued next page)

| May 5th | " | " | " | 1.50 | Payed* to date (*Miles' spelling). |
|---|---|---|---|---|---|
| May 14th | " | " | " | 1.30 | " " |
| May 18th | " | " | " | .10 | " " |
| May 19th | " | " | " | .10 | " " |
| Total dual (all with C.P.) | " | | " | 15.24 | |
| May 19th | | | | .12 | Solo " |
| May 22nd | Avro | G-EATU | Aerodrome | .10 | Solo |
| May 22nd | " | " | " | .05 | " " |
| Page total brought fwd.15.51 | | | | | |
| May 22nd | " | " | " | .09 | " " |
| May 22nd | " | " | " | .08 | |
| May 23rd | " | " | " | .10 | " " |
| May 23rd | " | " | " | .12 | " " |
| May 24thCentaur G-EALL | " | " | " | .04 | Dual |
| May 24th | " | " | " | .10 | Solo |
| May 24th | " | " | " | .10 | " " |
| May 24th | " | " | " | .0 | " " |
| Page total brought fwd. | | | " | 16.58 | " " |
| May 25th | " | " | " | .20 | " and etc... |

All subsequent flights in the Avro 504K and the Centaur 4A were made solo until on June 5th 1926, when a 5 minute flight was made in G-EALL with a passenger named "Poole" and it is possible that this was the name of the first passenger he carried. After this, F.G. Miles started carrying passengers regularly in the Centaur.

For the record the Avro 504K G-EATU was previously s/n E 3045. Originally registered to C.L. Pashley, Shoreham, it changed ownership in 1927 to the Gnat Aero Co., Shoreham and it crashed on the South Downs (exact location and date not known) prior to its C. of A. expiry on 22nd August 1928. Registration marks cancelled in January 1929.

The Central Centaur 4A(203) G-EALL was acquired by the Gnat Aero and Motor Co., Shoreham in May 1926 after a period of storage at Northolt. It was later scrapped and the registration marks cancelled in April 1930.

**SOUTHERN AEROPLANE CLUB,** Shoreham.
Formed:     1925
Membership: 46 (21 flying)
President:   Cdr. Sir A. Cooper Rawson MP, RNVR
Secretary:   Cecil A. Boucher
Instructors: Cecil L. Pashley (Aviator's Cert. 106, B Licence 529)
Frederick G. Miles (Aviator's Cert. 9003, B Licence 810)
Aircraft: Avro 504Ks G-EATU and G-EBJE
(Authors note: The absence of any reference to G-EAJU in this official record may be due to the fact that G-EAJU was written off by a Club member who made an unauthorised flight sometime in 1926, before lodgement of these details.)

# AIR ARMADA AT OFFICIAL AIRPORT OPENING

From the "Worthing Herald"   June 20th 1936

## "Happy Example of Joint Action by Local Authorities"

### —LORD SWINTON

## £60,000 PROJECT TO LINK SOUTH WITH CONTINENT

"I HOPE YOU WILL SET ON ITS JOURNEY AN UNDERTAKING WHICH, WHILE MARKING MUNICIPAL ENTERPRISE, DESERVES NATIONAL SUPPORT AND ENCOURAGEMENT."

With this invitation, made by Alderman F. W. A. Cushman, J.P. (Hove), chairman of the Brighton, Hove and Worthing Joint Municipal Airport Committee, the Mayors of Brighton (Councillor E. Denne), Hove (Councillor C. S. Loadsman), and Worthing (Alderman W. G. Tree) officially opened the new £60,000 airport at Shoreham on Saturday.

Gathering at the main entrance of the terminal building, Mr Stavers H. Tiltman, L.R.I.B.A. (hon. architect) presented each Mayor with a gold key.

### A MAE WEST-ISM

"You will now be able to come up and see us some time," he observed.

At the chairman's request Councillor Loadsman unlocked the door and Councillor Denne declared the airport open. He described the scheme as an amenity.

"I sincerely hope," he declared, "that the project will be a success. May the air traffic increase in the same way as the road traffic."

He then asked Alderman Tree to unveil a commemorative plaque in the entrance.

Speaking at the luncheon that preceded the opening Alderman Cushman extended a welcome on behalf of the three municipalities who are owners of the airport to visitors from Belgium, France, Germany and Holland.

### AIR MINISTER'S MESSAGE

"We had hoped," he said, "that we should have welcomed Lord Swinton, H.M. Minister of Air, but unfortunately we chose a day which has proved impossible for him. He has, however, been good enough to send us a message by which we are encouraged."

The message read: "I was greatly disappointed to be unable, through a long-standing engagement, to accept the invitation to open the Brighton, Hove and Worthing Joint Municipal Airport in person. I am very glad to have this opportunity of sending a message of encouragement and good wishes.

### FAR-SIGHTEDNESS

"An aerodrome may well become in the future as essential to a seaside town as a railway station. The municipalities of Brighton, Hove and Worthing are to be congratulated on their far-sightedness in realising this, and on their enterprise in establishing the joint airport.

" Rapid ground transport to and from the airport, which is an important consideration, is secured by the railway station alongside. Rapid communication by air with other parts of England is assured—thanks to the co-operation between the railway and air transport interests—by the twice-daily services which Railway Air Services, Ltd., are providing to a number of important centres.

" The airport is a happy example," the message continued, " of joint action by local authorities, and I heartily wish it success."

They had present, declared the chairman, Mr J. G. Gibson, who was officially representing Sir Francis Shelmerdine, the Director-General of Civil Aviation.

He congratulated Mr Stavers Tiltman, architect, who was entitled to the credit of constructing the airport. Mr Tiltman was also giving a handsome cup to the winner of the South Coast Air Challenge Trophy race.

" We had an inaugural meeting some eight or nine months ago," added Alderman Cushman, " when the airport was in an incomplete state, but sufficiently advanced for flying services to be operated.

## NO PROFIT FOR LONG TIME

" We have now completed our work of construction, and Brighton, Hove and Worthing have sunk some £60,000 in this scheme. To be quite frank, there is no hope of getting any cash return by way of profit for some years to come, but there are other considerations to take into account.

" We hear a good deal about amenities and publicity nowadays. Here, I think, we have an investment which is worth a good deal as being useful as well as ornamental in that this airport will ensure that Brighton, Hove and Worthing will be kept continually in the minds of the air-minded public—a public which we hope to see becoming larger in numbers as time goes on."

## LINK IN A CHAIN

They thought that the airport, he continued, would form an important link in the chain of similar projects throughout the country, and that commercial flying would become far more a part of everyday life than at present.

*It was possible to reach the Isle of Wight from the airport in 20 minutes, Bristol in 1¼ hours, Cardiff or Paris in 1½ hours, Dieppe and Deauville in 50 minutes, Ostend in 1¼ hours, Brussels in 1¼ hours, Amsterdam in 2¼ hours, and shortly regular services to all these places might be expected.*

Those services, he was confident, would be increased as time went on.

## WEEK-END SERVICES

" In addition," he remarked, " to what one might call 'set services' we want to encourage week-end and other excursions, both from home ports and abroad. I hope we shall not look in vain for the support of Chambers of Commerce and hotel proprietors, for it is obvious that the more traffic that can be attracted to this airport the more will be the benefit to the hotels and trade generally of our three towns."

The airport was equipped to receive any amount of traffic.

The control tower could be compared to the main signal box at a railway terminus. It was the most up-to-date in the country, with the possible exception of radio equipment, and this would probably be added within the course of a very few weeks.

There was also attached a flying school, a flying and social club, and a well-appointed restaurant—attractions which lent themselves to the social side.

Present at the luncheon were members of the three Corporations, the Duchess of Bedford, Lord Amherst, M.C. (airport manager), Lord Semphill, Sir Harry and Lady Preston, Captain Olley (managing director of Olley Air Services), Mr M. H. Volk (Hon. Aeronautical Adviser), Captain H. Duncan Davis, A.F.C., Mr P. E. Harvey, O.B.E. (Hon. Surveyor), Mr T. J. Owen (clerk and solicitor to Airport Committee) and Dr G. P. Smith, in addition to Continental pilots and friends.

## PAST AND PRESENT CRAFT

The pageant which succeeded the opening was a comprehensive demonstration of aircraft development in recent years. Both ancient and modern aircraft were displayed, including the pre-War Caudron, flown by Mr Ken Waller (Chief Instructor at Brooklands), who brought the machine from Brussels.

Mr Waller was, it will be recalled, third with Mr Cathcart Jones in the Mildenhall to Melbourne air race and the hero of the epic return flight from Brussels to Leopoldsville in the Belgian Congo.

Crazy flying by Mr Cecil Pashley (Chief Instructor, South Coast Flying Club) opened the proceedings, and other displays consisted of a parade of civil aircraft, an aerobatic display by Mr S. A. Thorn, the prominent test pilot, and a demonstration of the latest direct control autogiro by Mr R. A. C. Brie.

## INTERNATIONAL AIR RACE

Formation aerobatics by No. 19 (Fighter) Squadron, R.A.F., and demonstrations of ultra-light craft, formation flying and aerobatics by instructors of Brooklands Reserve Training School, a bombing competition by Max Findlay (Brooklands), Cecil Pashley (Shoreham) and Flight-Lieutenant I. Mackenzie (Sywell), and a parachute descent by Mr Gwyn John completed the display.

The final of the South Coast Air Challenge Trophy race was flown on the Sunday and resulted in a close duel between two Aeronca planes flown by J. D. Kirwin (West Australia) and Flying Officer A. Clausten (Farnborough).

Clausten eventually won with an average speed of 83¾ miles an hour, W. Humble (Doncaster) came in second, registering an average speed of 174 miles an hour, and Kirwin took third place, his average speed being 79½ miles an hour.

The prizes were subsequently distributed, after a continuation of the air pageant, by Mrs Duncan Davis.

The winner of the sealed time arrival competition on Saturday morning, when spectators witnessed the appearance of about one hundred machines, was won by Mr S. W. Ogden (Lympne), of the Cinque Ports Flying Club, who received £50.

Famous personalities attending the two days' display were Tommy Rose, Sir Alliott Roe, the inventor of the Avro machine, and Jim Mollison.

The excellent arrangements were entrusted to Mr B. S. Smallman (secretary, South Coast Flying Club) and Mr C. G. Browne (Advertising and Publicity Manager), and Mr A. Golding Barrett (Aerodrome Control Officer).

## THE " FLYING DACHSHUND "

Saturday's official opening at the municipal airport was a veritable "air circus." First spectators saw a performance of a "Flying Flea" and later they were entertained by a "Flying Dachshund."

A pet dog became air-minded and, although chased by airport officials and spectators when it intruded on to the landing ground, it eventually gained its objective.

"Dach" was forgotten for the time being.

The first 'plane home in the first heat of the South Coast Air Trophy race was arriving; the public prepared to congratulate the pilot but to their amazement out jumped "Dach," having travelled round the 48-mile course with his master, Flying-Officer A. C. Clauston, of Farnborough, at an average speed of 84½ miles an hour.

# APPENDIX PART 3

List of 277 Squadron aircraft recorded at Shoreham in 1944, from Sqn. Ldr. Len Healey's War Diary. Not all were necessarily based at Shoreham all the time, as there appears to have been a good deal of aircraft movement between the other 277 airfields at Hawkinge and Gravesend. Maximum complement of 277 Squadron Spitfires at Shoreham is believed to have been around 17. (Full serial numbers are omitted on occasions, and later in the Diary Len Healey just used identification letters like "N" Nuts, and no serial No. is quoted.)

| Spitfires | | Walrus | Sea Otters | Lysanders | Tiger Moth | Oxford | Master |
|-----------|--------|--------|-----------|-----------|------------|--------|--------|
| P 7911 | P 7490 | X 9847 | JM 770 | V 9487 | NL 693 | 644 | 569 |
| P 8020 | BL 666 | 89 | JM 796 | V 9545 | | | |
| P 7376 | P 7666 | 35 | 798 | | | | |
| P 8261 | P 7359 | LZ 315 | 745 | | | | |
| P 7605 | P 7917 | AD 917 | V 9865 | | | | |
| P 7734 | P 8216 | 936 | 802 | | | | |
| P 8030 | P 8479 | 912 | 59 | | | | |
| P 9261 | PM 522 | 9545 | | | | | |
| P 7911 | W 3528 | 914 | | | | | |
| P 7325 | 919 | 877 | | | | | |
| P 7675 | 163 | W 2248 | | | | | |
| P 7525 | AD199 | | | | | | |
| P 7673 | P 8761 | | | | | | |
| 445 | BM 510 | | | | | | |
| BM 273 | AD 105 | | | | | | |

# APPENDIX PART 4

Major notifiable accidents over the last 32 years:

March 13th 1964: The first accident in the history of the Southern Aero Club occurred when Tiger moth G-AKXO hit the top branches of a tree and crashed in the front garden of 77 Buckingham Road, Shoreham. The 23 year old pilot, Colin Barrett, and his passenger, Harold Ginn, were killed.

January 5th 1965: A Bölkow 107 from Shoreham crashed in the sea, killing Donald Jarvis, CFI at Sussex Flying Training Facilities, and his British Guianan pupil, Peter Phillips.

August 11th 1968: During a Tiger Club display, Arnold Green was flying a Turbulent in a balloon-bursting display over the airfield, when a balloon caught up in his wing and acted as a spoiler. The aircraft crashed killing the pilot.

May 8th 1970: Robert Sharpe, a crop-spraying pilot, took off from Golding Barn Farm in a Piper Pawnee 235. A cow ran in front of him and knocked off a wheel, so Sharp decided to make a one wheel landing at Shoreham. He survived; the cow did not.

January 6th 1972: Brighton ice-show skater, Frederick (Ricky) Wright was killed in a Bölkow Junior when he hit a power line in fog near Godalming.

August 11th 1978: There was another Turbulent crash during a Tiger Club display, but the pilot, John Harper, lived.

October 11th 1978: Captain Peter Stanton, a British Air Tours pilot, and Captain Patrick Hope of Dan Air, were killed when the Cessna 152 they had hired crashed in the sea off The Half Brick on Worthing sea front.

March 12th 1979: An Edinburgh policeman, PC Gilbert Shaw, and his passenger, ex-Flt. Lt. Thomas Moffat were flying from Turnhouse to Shoreham when they sent out a Mayday near the

Portslade power station. The pilot managed to avoid kerosene tanks in the harbour, but both he and his passenger were killed when the aircraft crashed on a grass embankment.

August 1st 1980: Anthony Roads and Peter Cramer, flying a Jodel G-AVIU from Shoreham to the Isle of Wight, crashed on a golf course and were killed.

January 12th 1981: John Cromwell-Morgan, aged 68, was seriously injured when he crash-landed his Fournier RF.4D 1,200 cc motor-glider by the A27 when he lost power on take-off. He died in hospital three months later.

December 15th 1981: Peter Roberts of Guernsey took off from Shoreham for Norwich in a Piper Aztec; his starboard engine failed and a wing tip hit the ground. The aircraft was a write-off, but the pilot was unhurt.

July 9th 1983: Keith Wickenden, until recently MP for Dorking, took-off in his Sea Devon to test a reconditioned engine. However the aircraft lost power and crashed on the bank of the River Adur just north of the A27 and burst into flames. The pilot died.

February 11th 1985: David Regi, a former Dan Air pilot, took-off from Shoreham in a Cessna 172 en route for Jersey. He sent out a Mayday near Alderney but he was not seen again. Over a year later a fishing boat recovered wreckage from his plane.

Sepember 19th 1988: A Jodel D.120 from Shoreham crashed just short of the landing strip at Wellcross Grange, Slinfold killing the owner-pilot Bodo Kaldenberg and his passenger Derek Alldi.

June 29th 1989: A four-seater Beechcraft Musketeer of Martlets Flying Group at Shoreham was carrying out an aerial survey of Langley Point, when it crashed on Eastbourne beach, injuring the pilot, Desmond de Bank, and his two passengers, Sidney Drew and Douglas Eldrett.

November 20th 1994: A Cessna 185 flying from Holland to Shoreham crashed at High Salvington, killing the pilot Michael McGrath and his passenger Mrs. Iris White. A third occupant, Barry Lamoon survived with injuries.

March 2nd 1996: A Jodel D.9 flown by Malcolm Allen suffered engine failure on approach to Shoreham. He skillfully avoided houses only to crash into a nearby field, and sadly lost his life.

SAMPLES OF LETTERS TO THE EDITOR OF THE "EVENING ARGUS" ON THE SUBJECT OF SHOREHAM AIRPORT. THE FIRST APPEARED ON NOV. 2nd 1995, AND THE OTHERS IN REPLY APPEARED IN NOV. 6TH ISSUE.

THERE they go again. Do you hear them? Wave after wave, of droning, noisy annoyance. Deafening pollution above our heads, day after insufferable day.

It seems that anyone with a spare ninety quid for a lesson is entitled to fly a small aircraft over my house and wherever I go within the proximity of Shoreham Airport. To make as much irritating engine sound as they wish and to put us all at risk of our sanity, or even our lives.

Circuits and bumps above Sompting and Lancing, without regard to the rights of anyone else to a quiet existence.

These trainee pilots are a threat, by flying over such a densely populated residential area, and are an accident just waiting to happen.

The Argus has regularly reported stories over the years of forced landings and pilots too ill or too old to fly. Yet no one takes a blind bit of notice.

These planes take off on a circuitous route over the Downs and they are obliged to remain within sight of the A27 and the sea. That is precisely where we all live and are forced to endure the noise and danger posed by these rich men's toys. I am heartily fed up with it and I imagine so are many other people.

I gather the three councils who own Shoreham Airport (meaning the public who pay for it out of Council Taxes) are delighted to have declared a profit for the first time in fifty years. Then it was only a measly £40,000 or so.

Sufficient proof it seems, to extend the activities at Shoreham to cargo planes.

Just mention the mere possibility of "job creation" and that's enough to justify anything out of the public purse.

Just how much of that so-called profit was actually paid from one local authority, such as the police authority for the helicopter, to the others? How much was actually from trading receipts – not much, I wager. Hardly a success story, is it?

Cargo aircraft and any other kind of flying machine can land readily enough at Gatwick and Stansted. We don't want them over our houses, on our doorsteps or in our living rooms, day after day.

The police helicopter has proved that it can land on a pocket handkerchief. So there must be an equally convenient site for it, if Shoreham Airport is closed for good.

Anyone with ego to spare for a flying lesson, can afford to go elsewhere. They should not be flying at our expense.

**F.R.R., Sompting**

IT seems to be the turn of Shoreham Airport again to receive criticism.

But the airport has been there for some 80 years, long before Messrs F.R.R. of Sompting (*November 2*) and Adam Trimingham (*same edition*) were born.

What were they doing when they looked round their present houses before they purchased them? Did they look round them at night? Was it foggy? Were they wearing blindfolds?

I can only suggest that they move out of the area, although I suspect that they are the types that if they moved to the country would only complain about the cocks crowing and the cattle lowing.

**Michael Rigby**

**Chester Avenue,**

**Lancing**

PERHAPS F.R.R. of Sompting was frightened by a dirigible at birth as this utter hatred for aviation and Shoreham Airport in particular must stem from somewhere.

Apparently trainee pilots are a threat to the local residents' sanity and even their lives are at risk from we pilots in our rich men's toys, referring to occasional stories of forced landings.

Student pilots are each accompanied by an experienced instructor until they reach solo standard – which means that not only can the student fly the aircraft safely in normal conditions but also in the event of an emergency, the worst and most unlikely case being an engine failure.

When this happens the aircraft simply becomes a glider and will be landed in the most convenient open space – it does not just drop out of the sky on to the nearest house.

As for being a rich man's sport, while recreational flying is not the cheapest of pastimes it has to be said that nearly all the students, far from being wealthy and looking for a flashy hobby, are in fact incredibly dedicated people.

I don't know where the idea of aeroplanes being obliged to remain in sight of the A27 and the sea came from, either – utter rubbish.

I have little sympathy for anyone complaining about aircraft noise at one of the UK's oldest airports, so please stop telling us we have huge egos and come and see us. We're remarkably friendly.

**Toby Dixon**

**Assistant Instructor,**

**Airbase Flying Club**

IT would seem F.R.R. is the classic whinging, whining and disruptive community pain that we all grow to hate so much. The type of person who spends most of the day looking around to see what they can complain about.

Where is there a better place to fly small aeroplanes than from a place where for 180 degree of the operation airspace, flying takes place over the sea?

Tell this killjoy to get a life. I live one mile from the end of the runway at Gatwick. However, I respect people's right to fly and the airport was here before I was.

**Hamish Neathercoat**

**Langshott, Horley**

F.R.R.'s remark concerning unfit pilots reflects a degree of ignorance concerning the medical requirements necessary to fly an aircraft. These are quite stringent and medical examinations take place with increasing frequency as pilots get older.

As to the general level of risk, the third-party risk from all forms of flying is minute compared to driving.

General aviation has become increasingly marginalised in recent years, both as a result of airspace restrictions and due to closure of a number of airfields – often as a result of emotive campaigns by vested interests. It would be a tragedy if this should be allowed to happen here.

**Alastair Brand**

**University of Sussex**

IT would be as absurd to fly a light aircraft from Gatwick, as suggested, as it would be to attempt to land an Airbus at Shoreham.

Those who call for the closure of the airport will be delighted to know that where this has happened elsewhere the sites are generally turned into industrial parks or housing estates.

**M.F. Bowles**

**Kingsway, Hove**

IF F.R.R. moved to Sompting since about 1911 then I feel no sympathy as there has been an airfield at Shoreham almost since Pontius was a Pilot!

Shoreham is the oldest active aerodrome in Great Britain and long may it stay that way.

**Terry R. Kearney**

**Hillcrest Drive,**

**Ashington**

# INDEX